CONTINUING
LA CAUSA

LATINOS:
EXPLORING DIVERSITY AND CHANGE

CONTINUING

LA CAUSA

Organizing Labor in California's Strawberry Fields

Gilbert Felipe Mireles

FIRST**FORUM**PRESS

A DIVISION OF LYNNE RIENNER PUBLISHERS, INC. • BOULDER & LONDON

Published in the United States of America in 2013 by
FirstForumPress
A division of Lynne Rienner Publishers, Inc.
1800 30th Street, Boulder, Colorado 80301
www.firstforumpress.com
www.rienner.com

and in the United Kingdom by
FirstForumPress
A division of Lynne Rienner Publishers, Inc.
3 Henrietta Street, Covent Garden, London WC2E 8L

Library of Congress Cataloging-in-Publication Data
Mireles, Gilbert Felipe.
  Continuing la causa: organizing labor in California's strawberry fields /
Gilbert Felipe Mireles.
(Latinos: exploring diversity and change)
Includes bibliographical references and index.
ISBN 978-1-935049-64-7 (hc : alk. paper)
  1. Migrant agricultural laborers—Labor unions—California. 2. Hispanic American agricul-
tural laborers—California. 3. Strawberry industry—Employees—California. 4. Labor
unions—Organizing—California. 5. United Farm Workers. I. Title.
HD6515.A29M57 2013
331.88'1347509794—dc23   2013013077

British Cataloguing in Publication Data
A Cataloguing in Publication record for this book
is available from the British Library.

This book was produced from digital files prepared by the author
using the FirstForumComposer.

Printed and bound in the United States of America

5 4 3 2 1

Para mis padres, Gilberto y Amelia,
por su amor, apoyo, y paciencia

Contents

Preface

As a child growing up in California's Central San Joaquin Valley, I learned about the United Farm Workers (UFW) and Cesar Chavez. Even at my young age, I could sense a mixed and complicated legacy. Certainly, there was a great deal of respect for the union and admiration for the man. My mother, who had first come to the United States in the 1970s, bitterly remembered having to use *el cortito*, a short-handled hoe favored by the industry but torturous to the backs of laborers, who had to stoop all day using it. Although she was never involved in the union, my mother knew that the UFW had succeeded in outlawing the pain-inducing implement. Various other aspects of farm labor had also improved due to the union's efforts. No longer were there as many horror stories of egregious contact with pesticides. Access to clean drinking water and latrines was now the norm. We all sensed that conditions in the fields had improved in recent years.

The reverence for Cesar Chavez was palpable for me when speaking with Mexican American students on my tours of universities like Fresno State and UC Berkeley as a college applicant. His image was prominently depicted on murals, and the UFW flag was proudly displayed wherever Mexican-origin students congregated. Born in Yuma, Arizona, Chavez was one of us. Like many of these students' parents, he had been a farm laborer who never strayed from his roots. His example inspired us Mexican Americans. But this iconography gave way to a different perspective for farmworkers in many of the small farming communities in California's Central Valley.

La union de Chávez, as the UFW was known to many Mexican immigrants, was not of any great significance in the lives of the farmworking families I knew in the 1980s. For many observers, the heyday of the union was in the past. Farmworkers were only remotely aware of the grape boycott that seemed so compelling to socially conscious urbanites. Most farmworkers only heard about the campaign secondhand, from relatives or friends living in the Salinas Valley, where the UFW was most active. They heard rumors of farmers being forced out of business or closing shop when the union tried to organize workers. Word traveled of fierce divisions emerging in workplaces between workers for and against unionization. Such disruptions seemed threatening to farm-worker households that lacked financial cushions. The workers weren't the docile, keep-your-head-down immigrants imagined by some people, but neither were they untapped political agents with a dormant class consciousness waiting to erupt with the right catalyst. Like many Americans, they were hardworking people focused on putting food on the table and enjoying their precious free time with their loved ones. Their work in the fields allowed them to do just that. The union was a faint part of these workers' consciousness.

I continued to cross paths with the UFW while in college and graduate school on the East Coast. Attending presentations on workers' rights, I marveled at the strength of an organization that could send delegations of workers to speak to audiences at elite colleges and universities thousands of miles from the fields of California. During my first year of graduate school in 1996, the UFW launched its strawberry-worker organizing campaign. Suddenly, the perfect opportunity had arisen to connect my interest in social movements with my personal experiences growing up in an agricultural community. Energized, I returned to the fields of California to research something with which I had been familiar all my life but which still remained a mystery: the UFW and immigrant farmworkers in the state. This study represents the outcome of that research.

Acknowledgments

This book has its roots in the Department of Sociology at Yale University. Chris Rhomberg and Joshua Gamson, both in Sociology, shared their time and insights on labor and social movements and offered helpful advice and constructive criticism. Debra Minkoff also played a pivotal role in my intellectual development by first introducing me to the study of social movements and encouraging my interests in the UFW. However, it was Gerald Jaynes, in the Department of Economics at Yale, who saw promise in the project and agreed to work with me. His insights on immigrants in the US labor market, as well as his guidance and encouragement, were invaluable during the initial phases of this project, and I am extremely grateful to him.

In California, I was fortunate to have made contact with Jonathan Fox and Paul Johnston, both scholars at UC Santa Cruz with an intimate understanding of immigrants and labor in the Pajaro Valley. They encouraged the project and provided thoughtful suggestions based on their local knowledge, pushing me to refine my thinking about the case. In Watsonville, my cousin Yakira Landaverry and her husband, Carlos, helped me transition into the local community. Yakira and Carlos introduced me to local attorney David Morales and his wife, Silvia, who graciously opened their home to me. It was through David that I came to know the local political scene. Also in Watsonville, I met Frank Bardacke, a true organic intellectual, who shared his knowledge and personal experience with farm work and organized labor in the local area. This was especially helpful to understanding the history of the UFW in the Pajaro Valley. I also learned a great deal about the local industry from Coastal Berry president Earnie Farley and local farmer Mike Dobler, who took a genuine interest in the project and provided valuable information about farming and labor on the Central Coast. I am indebted to Vicente Morales and Rosendo Rodriguez, who shared their experiences as workers in the Central Coast agriculture industry and helped me understand the complexities of the Mexican immigrant experience. I would also like to thank Jaime Juarez and Jayesh Patel, who generously subsidized my life as a poor graduate student in the Bay Area. Raquel Hug similarly helped, by always being willing to share a bottle of wine and words of encouragement.

This book was completed at Whitman College, and I am very grateful to the Sociology Department there. Bill Bogard, Keith Farrington, Michelle Janning, and Helen Kim have been wonderful colleagues who are collegial, supportive, and encouraging. I am also extremely grateful to the college for its generous funding and especially to Tim Kaufman-Osborn, provost and dean of faculty, for his continued support of this project. Here I should note that provost staff Sally Hooker, Karen Zollman, and Susan Bennett ensured that the necessary bureaucratic procedures associated with that support functioned smoothly and efficiently. A special thanks is due to Ken Worthy, who reviewed the manuscript closely and offered helpful advice on the structure and substance of this book. I would also like to thank the anonymous reviewers who took time out of their busy schedules to carefully read earlier versions of my manuscript and offer very useful suggestions for improvement. It is important to note, of course, that the arguments presented in the book are my own and don't necessarily represent the views of the various readers who kindly offered comments and suggestions.

Finally, and most important, I am grateful to the people of Watsonville, who made me feel welcome—and especially to the farmworkers who were willing to tell me their stories. I sincerely hope that this book will be of service to them.

1

The United Farm Workers

The United Farm Workers of America (UFW) features prominently in the modern American labor movement and in the struggles for racial justice among minority groups in the United States. The lives of American farmworkers have been greatly improved through the union's efforts. Both the UFW and Cesar Chavez are central to understanding the Mexican American experience in the United States.[1] Both are revered. The history of the union is not, however, one of unequivocal success. The late 1970s through the early 1990s were a period of dormancy for the UFW, with little active organizing taking place. The situation changed in 1993 with the death of Cesar Chavez. After assuming leadership of the organization, Chavez's son-in-law Arturo Rodriguez embarked on a series of organizing campaigns to revitalize the union and continue *la causa*; the struggle for farmworker justice. In 1996 the UFW initiated its largest campaign in decades as it attempted to organize workers in the California strawberry industry. This book chronicles that campaign and explains the initial failures and eventual success of the union.

The strawberry campaign took place during a period when issues of labor and immigration were dominating headlines in California. As many commentators discussed the decline of organized labor in the United States, unions were enjoying success and even resurgence in California. The Service Employees International Union's (SEIU) 1990 Justice for Janitors campaign had resulted in a significant gain for organized labor in California. Unionization campaigns by the Hotel Employees and Restaurant Employees Union (HERE) and other unions were also meeting with success.[2] What these campaigns had in common was that it was immigrants who were being organized. To many insiders, California in the 1990s seemed like the wave of the future for unions, with immigrants forming the basis of the resurgence of organized labor.

The possibility of resurgence had significant implications for local and state politics in California. Unions have always been active participants in California politics. Various labor councils and locals have courted allied politicians and supported legislation in the state. Examples abound. During the 2001 mayoral race in Los Angeles, the local County Federation of Labor endorsed labor-friendly Democratic candidate Antonio Villaraigosa. This umbrella for the city's numerous unions not only provided financial support for the race but also volunteered 2,500 workers for door-to-door campaigning.[3] Another example is the Citizenship Project, the Teamsters-affiliated organization that worked to increase the civic participation of immigrant workers in their local communities. These political connections typify the close relations between institutional politics and organized labor in California and demonstrate how unions have facilitated the civic incorporation of immigrants into American society.

However, not everything was rosy for immigrants and their supporters. The increasing militarization of the US-Mexico border was a well-known fact courtesy of Spanish-language media outlets. This made an already difficult trip to and from Mexico even more difficult for immigrants without proper documentation. Compounding these difficulties, in 1994 California voters passed Proposition 187, intended to deny basic government services to undocumented California residents. Proposition 187 faced legal challenges and was eventually found unconstitutional in federal court. Still, anti-immigrant sentiment lingered. For many immigrants, the hostile environment was reason to retract from public life and keep a low profile. The tragic events of September 11, 2001, only made life more difficult for Californians perceived as foreigners. Labor resurgence and anti-immigrant sentiment stood as the socio-political backdrop to the UFW's unionization campaign in the strawberry industry.

During the 1990s, however, organized labor did not consider immigration status as an obstacle to unionization. Large and successful unionization drives among immigrant workers in the state during the first half of the decade had upended conventional wisdom that immigrants could not be organized. A common refrain heard in labor circles at the time was that immigrants should be organized "as workers, not as immigrants" (Johnston 2001). Neither the UFW nor the AFL-CIO considered that legal status might impede the organization of farmworkers. Both organizations viewed the strawberry campaign as the start of an ambitious plan to organize immigrant workers in different industries across the entire state.[4]

When I arrived in California in the summer of 2000 to study immigrant farmworker mobilization, the UFW campaign was winding down.[5] To the surprise of many observers, an upstart group of anti-UFW workers calling themselves El Comité de Trabajadores de Coastal Berry (Coastal Berry Farmworkers Committee, usually referred to simply as the Comité) had beat the UFW three times in state-sponsored elections. After extended legal maneuvering, a judge ruled that the UFW would represent workers in southern work areas and the Comité would be the bargaining agent for workers in Coastal Berry's Northern California operations. It was an uneasy peace that did not last long. In 2002, when the Comité's contract was up for renewal, the UFW challenged them and easily won the election to represent workers in Coastal Berry's Northern California operations. When I initially began to study this case, I was intrigued by what seemed like a great sociological puzzle. Prevailing social movement perspectives would have predicted a clear and outright victory by the UFW in its initial efforts to unionize the strawberry workers. Instead, the UFW was thwarted by a loosely organized group of anti-union workers.

The case of the UFW at Coastal Berry defied common understandings of how social movements succeed. Here was a seasoned organization that was extremely well-organized and in command of an impressive range of material, political, and symbolic resources. California had a Democratic governor and legislature. The UFW has historically had close ties to both. The union also enjoyed close ties to national Democrats and national labor leaders. Impressively enough, the UFW had been able to get the largest strawberry producer in the nation sold to union-friendly investors—ample testament to its expansive ties and political leverage. No unionization campaign is ever easy, and the agriculture industry in California has always proven itself a formidable challenger. But if ever a union was well-positioned to win a campaign, this was it. Yet somehow a rag-tag group of workers at Coastal Berry, with no resources or political clout, managed to surprise everyone and beat the UFW not once but three times. This unfolding of events simply didn't make sense to a sociologist studying social movements. Something peculiar was happening, and I was determined to figure out what it was.

The UFW and its supporters claimed that the Comité was an industry front-group. Certainly, there was reason to suspect that it was. Early in the campaign, the UFW had uncovered incontrovertible evidence of grower-financed anti-union groups operating in the Central Coast. But subsequently Coastal Berry was sold to union-friendly investors, and it was unlikely that the new owners would support anti-union efforts at the company. In fact, they had purchased Coastal Berry specifically to provide an ownership that would be neutral in the unionization campaign. Perhaps other growers in the local strawberry industry were responsible, but by now the early anti-union financiers were embroiled in serious litigation with the UFW, and it seemed that a chastened grower community was unlikely to engage in further shenanigans. For these reasons, I was skeptical of the claim that the Comité was an industry-driven effort. I sought evidence to the contrary, but none was ever found—by me, other researchers, or the UFW.

It would be easy to dismiss the Comité as a company union. The group certainly counted among its leaders several supervisors, foremen, and other employees of the company. But one cannot dismiss the fact that the group had won three consecutive state-sponsored elections. In each election the majority of workers at Coastal Berry had chosen to throw their lot in with the Comité rather than the more sophisticated and professional UFW, and it was not immediately apparent why. The Comité demanded serious scholarly inquiry if I were to make sense of what happened in the California strawberry industry between 1996 and 2003.

The UFW chose to focus on the Coastal Berry Company after close consultation with the AFL-CIO. As a subsidiary of the Monsanto Corporation, Coastal Berry made an attractive target for a variety of reasons (to be explained in Chapter 6). This strategy was the result of a "corporate campaign" approach popular among labor unions in the 1980s and 1990s. In a corporate campaign, labor unions use detailed industry research to decide how best to organize a particular employer or industry sector. This approach had proven effective in the past, but as the strawberry campaign demonstrates, it is imperfect.

Developed and implemented by sophisticated organizations, corporate campaigns emphasize organization-level analyses in their approach to unionization campaigns. By focusing on employers as organizations, however, this approach runs the risk of de-emphasizing worker views and interests. Among immigrant workforces like those found in the California strawberry industry, patron-client relations are often structured in a way that exerts tremendous power over workers. When it focused on Coastal Berry's upper management as the major impediment to unionization, the UFW failed to fully recognize and act on foremen and supervisors, who were the major power brokers among the company workforce and who stood to lose the most from a successful unionization campaign. When organizing from above, as the UFW did in this case, unions risk not fully accounting for micro-level dynamics that influence individual decision-making processes.

My field research revealed that the success of the Comité was due to the strength of patron-client relations found within family and family-like networks. It was through one-on-one exchanges among family and close friends that the Comité was able to gain the support of a majority of workers at Coastal Berry. In the end, however, the strength of interpersonal bonds alone was not enough to win the unionization campaign. The UFW ultimately prevailed because of what I call *organizational capacity*—a characteristic of fully developed formal organizations that allows one organization to meet its interests over and against the interests of others with which it interacts. Organizational capacity facilitates the acquisition and implementation of institutional knowledge. Institutions are the rules that dictate interorganizational dynamics. All organizations must contend with institutions as they attempt to meet their objectives in an environment comprising other competing and allied organizations. For example, California's Agricultural Labor Relations Act (ALRA), which governs the rights and responsibilities of employers and employees in the state's agriculture industry, is an institution. It regulates the behavior of labor and capital interests, and is itself the outcome of interactions between labor and capital interests.

If social movements are to make lasting social change that is structural in nature, they must have an understanding of institutions and be able to interact with and shape them in their favor. One of the reasons that the National Association for the Advancement of Colored People (NAACP) has been so successful in its long history is that it developed and sustained an organizational capacity that allowed it raise effective legal challenges to racial injustice in the United States. These challenges would not have succeeded without knowledge of American jurisprudence and the ability to operate within the legal system.

However, social change through institutional mechanisms poses challenges for social movement organizations. Groups that focus on change at the institutional level risk alienating themselves from the population base that originally gives rise to collective action. Recall that the unionization campaign began in the fields but ended in the courts. The ability to operate within the legal system required a cadre of specially trained practitioners—lawyers. The problem for the NAACP, as well as the UFW, is that however effective these skilled practitioners may be at bringing about structural social change because of their knowledge of arcane institutional procedures, those skills don't necessarily translate into grassroots support for the movement. Moreover, in their reliance on lawyers and other such highly specialized professionals, social movement organizations run the risk of becoming technocratic organizations operated with little interaction with the very people on whose behalf they are ostensibly working. This is what happened to the UFW in the 1980s, after the union had moved its operations away from the agricultural centers of the San Joaquin and Salinas Valleys to the distant town of La Paz, in the Tehachapi Mountains. During that period the UFW concentrated on direct mailings to union supporters and boycott management and neglected farmworker organizing. The UFW's absence from the fields in the 1980s had significant consequences in the 1990s during the strawberry campaign.

The fact that the UFW has long become decoupled from its base has particularly troubling implications among a farmworker population made up predominantly of recent immigrants. Social movement organizations have historically functioned to ease the socio-political integration of marginalized groups into the mainstream of American society. Groups such as the League of United Latin American Citizens (LULAC) and the aforementioned NAACP have served the African American and Latino populations effectively in this manner. The UFW could greatly benefit immigrants and American society at large if it were to function in this way. The fact that it did not created significant obstacles in the strawberry campaign and does not bode well for the integration of society's newest members. The UFW's lack of engagement with farmworkers is especially troubling considering both the outsized role of organizations and the growing presence of immigrants in contemporary American society.

Thus, organizational capacity and patron-client relationships played major and alternating roles in the historical development of the strawberry campaign. Having organizational capacity but lacking social networks in California's strawberry fields, the UFW faced tremendous difficulty organizing workers at Coastal Berry. In contrast, patron-client relationships at the company operating within kinship networks allowed the Comité to undermine the union's overtures to workers. Organizational capacity ultimately gave the UFW the upper hand, however. The fact that it was able to finally win a union contract at the company is testament not to its abilities to organize immigrant farmworkers but rather to its position as a sophisticated organization with institutional prowess. The remainder of the book will elaborate on this thesis given the events surrounding the Coastal Berry campaign.

In the next chapter I walk the reader through the agricultural community of Watsonville, California, and survey the unique characteristic of the Pajaro Valley and the larger Central Coast region where the campaign took place. I also introduce some of the people whose lives were directly impacted by the UFW's unionization efforts. I provide background information on the campaign and explain the theoretical framework that I use to examine the case.

In Chapter 2 I provide a more detailed narrative account of the events in the California strawberry industry between 1996 and 2003. This chapter lays out the factual contours of the campaign, which are then analyzed in the remainder of the book. (Appendix B provides a timeline to help the reader keep track of the important events of the campaign.) In Chapter 4 I further explore why some workers were eager to side with the UFW but a majority were not. Using a framework that integrates a network theory view of the US labor market and that applies insights from extensive research on transnational immigrant networks in the western United States, I analyze the strawberry industry and examine how interactions among workers and farmers contributed to the emergence of a broad range of responses to the UFW campaign. The average immigrant working in the California strawberry fields is one part of an extensive web of interpersonal relationships spanning the job site, the local community, and his or her country of origin. I further explain industry-wide labor market dynamics and the specific dynamics within the Coastal Berry Company.

Chapter 5 discusses the organizational theories of Max Weber and others to explain why formal organizations such as the UFW are better at achieving structural social change than loosely organized groups such as the Comité. I review the significant features of formal organizations and develop organizational profiles of the dominant organizations in the campaign, including the Comité, the UFW, and Coastal Berry. These profiles help explain the Comité's forced shift from a network-based set of individual preferences to a loosely structured organizational vehicle ultimately incapable of engaging the UFW in an organizational field well known to the latter. My analysis reveals why it was only after workers had elected the Comité as their bargaining agent that the UFW was able to defeat the Comité. Once the unionization battle moved out of the fields and into the courts, the UFW was able to make use of its institutional capacity—a capacity that the Comité did not possess. Organizations, not networks, best accomplish the complex task of labor representation because they enable the navigation of institutional frameworks established to govern labor relations.

Chapter 6 presents a holistic analysis of the campaign by applying three concepts—networks, organizations, and institutions—to explain the Comité's initial successes and ultimate failure at Coastal Berry. Chapter 7 extends the discussion by examining institutional processes operating at the interorganizational level. A theory of institutions as "rules of the game" for interactions among organizations is presented and applied historically to explain the emergence of successful advocacy efforts among disenfranchised groups in society. I argue that an organization's knowledge of and ability to execute these rules represents a cultural competency not unlike the "cultural capital" invoked by scholars to explain individual capacities and predilections. We can attribute the Comité's failure to its lack of this institutional knowledge. Without knowing the intricacies of the ALRA or how to effectively engage the Labor Relations Board, there was no way the Comité could hope to outmaneuver the UFW.

The book concludes by considering the campaign's broader implications for American civil society and participatory democracy. The US democratic system may be thought of as a system that distributes power among a wide range of competing groups and individuals. A central tenet of this vision of government is the ability of individuals to participate in governance in the classic liberal-democratic sense. Yet as DeTocqueville tells us, in the United States this participation has usually taken an organizational form. The grip of organizations on society has strengthened in the nineteenth and twentieth centuries as economic interactions have come to dominate social life. This development raises interesting questions concerning the nature of individual participation in American society. It is especially troubling for the newest members of society when one considers how hard it can be for immigrants to learn to navigate in their new environment. It becomes an almost herculean task to acquire the formal rules of participation and the cultural competencies necessary to bring about meaningful social change. The strawberry campaign reveals that organizations that have developed the ability to navigate institutional processes can help immigrants become more socially engaged. Unfortunately, not all organizations that are supposed to serve immigrants operate in this way.

---

[1] In Spanish, the name *César Chávez* uses accent marks. However, most English-language writers omit these. Neither the Cesar E. Chavez Foundation nor the UFW use accent marks when referencing Chavez's name. I have followed their lead and omitted the accents found in the original Spanish. Throughout the text, I have employed accent marks on personal names when specifically asked to do so.

[2] In 2004 the HERE merged with the Union of Needletrades, Industrial, and Textile Employees (UNITE) to form UNITE HERE. A year later, in 2005, UNITE HERE left the AFL-CIO and joined the Change to Win Federation.

[3] Villaraigosa, a former labor organizer, narrowly lost the mayoral race to James Hahn in a run-off election. In an interesting turn of events, the County Federation of Labor had endorsed Hahn, not Villaraigosa, for mayor in the 2005 race. Justifying the shift, Federation official Miguel Contreras stated, "An old labor saying reminds us that labor rewards our friends" (*LA Weekly*, Dec. 31, 2004).

[4] In retrospect, it appears that by emphasizing the organizability of immigrants, labor leaders may have underestimated the significance of legal status. Johnston (2001) suggests that the era of amnesty and lax immigration enforcement in the late 1980s may have contributed to the false notion that immigration status was unimportant in labor mobilization. Johnston (2001) goes on to argue that citizenship concerns cannot be divorced from immigrant labor mobilization. This is especially important to keep in mind when we consider the fact that the strawberry campaign took place during a time of intense anti-immigrant sentiment. Had the UFW and the AFL-CIO taken legal status into account, they may have been able to better address the concerns of workers in the industry. It should be noted that since the 1990s, labor leaders have changed their stance with respect to immigration. In 2000 the AFL-CIO Executive Council officially reversed its previous support for sanctions against employers of unauthorized workers and called for a new amnesty program for undocumented workers. In 2006 organized labor was a central component of a nationwide coalition of groups that mobilized in support of immigrant rights.

[5] For an extended discussion on the methods used in this study, please refer to Appendix A at the end of the book.

2

The Drive to Organize

On a spring day in April 1997, the United Farm Workers of America (UFW) led a march of approximately 30,000 people through the streets of downtown Watsonville, California. Watsonville is a farm town of 44,000 inhabitants at the northern end of the state's Central Coast. The region's climate provides ideal conditions for berry cultivation, and commercial strawberry growing is a large part of the local economy. During the previous harvest season, pickers at some area farms had protested working conditions. In one instance, they called on the UFW to help them organize. However, not all worksites were the same, and farmworker opinions regarding the UFW and unionization varied significantly among the sites.

Several months later, in August 1997, another march was held in downtown Watsonville. This time, however, a group of about 3,500 farmworkers participated in a "March for Truth" to denounce the UFW and its organizing efforts. It was the second such event that summer. In the months before August, an organization called the Agricultural Workers Committee (AWC) had formed in the Pajaro Valley in response to the UFW's activities in the Watsonville area. Its primary objective was to educate workers about their rights regarding unionization. According to the group's leaders, most strawberry pickers did not want to unionize. Shortly thereafter, the UFW filed a lawsuit against several prominent growers, claiming that they had provided financial support for the activities of the anti-UFW activists.

Worker discontent was not simply the product of anti-UFW sentiment stoked by the growers. Despite grower support for some organizations, other workers' groups remained independent. At one company, they went on to form El Comité de Trabajadores de Coastal Berry (known simply as *el Comité* among the workers). This group eventually won three major state-sanctioned elections against the UFW, which enabled it to thwart that union's early efforts to organize in the sector. It took the UFW five years and several million dollars to finally overcome the Comité and gain full recognition from the state as the exclusive bargaining agent for the company's workers. In this book, I investigate the peculiar course of events that led to worker resistance against unionization and the ultimate success of the UFW. As I show, the UFW employed a top-down, organization-centered approach to the campaign, which failed to adequately account for the role of clientelistic relations within the company workforce. However, the initial strength of workers' social networks was eventually overcome by the power of the UFW, whose organizational capacity and institutional awareness allowed it to navigate the complexities of labor law and public relations to gain a foothold in the strawberry industry.

A Rocky Path to Unionization

The 1997 march through Watsonville came at the beginning of a sophisticated and well-organized unionization drive. The UFW claimed to have rallied 30,000 people, although the number determined by the local officials was lower: 17,000. According to local newspaper accounts, roughly 20,000 workers toiled in California's strawberry fields under difficult conditions with minimal pay. In a UFW report, "Five Cents for Fairness: The Case for Change in the Strawberry Fields," the public learned that the state's strawberry industry grossed $450 million per year. At the same time, strawberry pickers made, on average, an annual wage between $9,000 and $12,000. Some workers were clearly unhappy with the inequity of the situation. In 1995, workers at VCNM Farms in neighboring Salinas Valley had held a wildcat strike. In that instance, the growers decided to "disk" their fields and claim bankruptcy rather than recognize a non-state-sanctioned election in which workers voted 332 to 50 in favor of UFW representation.[1]

The UFW demonstrated tremendous organizational skill in its efforts to unionize the California strawberry industry. Getting tens of thousands of people together to march for a social cause is only one example of the union's success in this respect. To organize the march, the UFW had to secure the support of other labor organizations and their members, as well as coordinate activities with a wide range of public and private entities at the local, state, and national levels. Furthermore, the UFW was able to publicize this event to a broad audience by releasing well-written, informative press releases in local, state, and national media outlets. The message presented to the international press corps that day in April was clear: things had to change in the strawberry industry.[2]

The campaign came at a time of transition for the UFW. The charismatic Cesar Chavez had recently passed away, and his son-in-law, Arturo Rodriguez, had become union president. Exercising pragmatism and management skills, Rodriguez quickly led the union to craft a well-conceived plan to organize workers in the strawberry industry. The UFW employed several strategies to pressure individual growers, growers' groups, and the entire industry to facilitate union formation in a campaign of a type that labor studies scholars call a "corporate campaign." The union was also able to secure financial and human resources from the AFL-CIO. Drawing on successes in the 1990s among groups such as the Service Employees International Union (SEIU) and the Hotel Employees and Restaurant Employees Union (HERE), the AFL-CIO began to focus on organizing immigrant workers, particularly in the western states. In those campaigns, the unions employed researchers to gather strategically useful information about individual employers and entire industries. The UFW strawberry campaign also made use of such researchers. Furthermore, the AFL-CIO tie enabled the UFW to place dozens of organizers in the fields and in workers' homes.[3] To add pressure to the industry, the UFW staged highly publicized events, including folk concerts and celebrity arrests. The union was also able to negotiate highly publicized pledges from large supermarket chains to honor workers' rights to organize. One of the nonbinding agreements was made with the Safeway chain of stores, a longtime foe. The arrangement did not entail the removal of berries from market shelves, but Safeway and the UFW issued joint press releases to alert the public about labor relations in the industry. The union also enjoyed strong political support. In July 1998, at a labor convention in Oakland, Senator Barbara Boxer and Democratic gubernatorial candidate Gray Davis pledged their support to labor in the state.[4]

In June 1997, in perhaps the strongest showing of its formidable organizational ability, the UFW, with the help of the AFL-CIO, secured the sale of the largest strawberry company in the nation to pro-union investors. The original owner, Monsanto Corporation, sold its Gargiulo Company to two investors from Maryland, Landon Butler and David Gladstone, who had close ties to organized labor and the Democratic Party, and renamed the company Coastal Berry.[5]

The sale was a coup for the UFW. Soon after assuming control, Coastal Berry's owners wrote a letter to the company's approximately 1,500 pickers, informing them that they respected their right to organize and would not interfere with the organizing campaign. If the UFW could win a contract there, it would have a secure foothold from which to organize the 20,000 workers in the entire strawberry industry. That spring, the union began in earnest a grassroots strategy of labor mobilization. This strategy ultimately failed to break the power of foremen and supervisors at the company, who had the most to lose from a successful organizing campaign.

For its part, the grower community quickly mobilized several responses to the UFW's actions. Employing a creative legal strategy, the Western Growers Association (WGA) sued Coastal Berry, claiming that the company had broken a union-neutrality agreement. According to the Ventura County–based growers' association, Landon Butler and David Gladstone, in a letter to workers dated April 1998, expressed a pro-UFW stance, thus violating neutrality. However, an Agricultural Labor Relations Board (ALRB) judge dismissed the suit.

Meanwhile, as workers across the industry were organizing, in the early stages of that campaign growers were hiring *consultantes* to facilitate the development of anti-union organizations.[6] These organizations and consultants were tasked with "educating" captive worker audiences about unions, and in fact managed to inspire thousands of laborers to march against the UFW in the spring 1997 demonstration. When the UFW discovered a paper trail connecting these groups to several growers, it quickly filed lawsuits. The UFW succeeded in putting an end to the activities of these anti-union groups, but not before workers in the industry had absorbed their arguments against labor unions and the role of the ALRB in California agriculture.

The following season, during the UFW's second year of organizing at Coastal Berry, the Comité appeared from within the middle ranks of the company hierarchy. In July, the quasi-union filed an election petition with the ALRB, asking for an election. Unlike the rules of the National Labor Relations Act, California's Agricultural Labor Relations Act stipulates that elections must be held within seven days of such filings. The short time frame set in motion a rapid legal response in which the UFW filed multiple objections to the election. When the objections were dismissed, the union abstained from the election in protest. Workers at the company were presented with a ballot that listed two options: the Comité or no union. The Comité won. However, the election outcome was later nullified due to procedural errors based on meticulous legal arguments presented by the UFW. The Comité and its supporters expressed frustration that their wishes had not been respected.

A year later, in June 1999, the Comité again petitioned for an election, and this time the UFW was on the ballot. Again, workers voted in favor of the Comité. The election results were supposed to have designated it as the sole bargaining agent of Coastal Berry's 1,500 workers, but the UFW vigorously protested the election results in the courts and in the press. Almost a year passed before a final ruling was made. During that time, the company was losing money, management changed, and production declined. Relations among workers with different affiliations were tense. The UFW, the Comité, Coastal Berry, and the ALRB filed competing motions in the courts.

In March 2000, almost a year after the election, a ruling was issued. ALRB administrative law judge Thomas Sobel decreed that Coastal Berry be designated as two distinct bargaining units. The UFW would represent workers in the company's Southern California operation (about one-fourth of Coastal Berry's production), and the Comité would be the bargaining agent for the northern operation. Both unions agreed to this arrangement. In 2002, the UFW filed a petition to organize Coastal Berry's Northern California operation, then went on to handily beat the Comité and consolidate its control as the sole bargaining agent at the company. In 2004, Coastal Berry was sold to the Dole Food Company. Along with Swanton Berry Farms in northern Santa Cruz County, Coastal Berry remains one of only two berry producers under union contract.

Geography and Social Ethos

California's strawberry industry is centered around the idyllic Monterey Bay on the state's Central Coast. At the northern end of the bay is the city of Santa Cruz; roughly twenty-five miles to the south is the city of Monterey. On a clear day in Santa Cruz, one can look south across the ocean to see the southern tip of the bay. Between the two cities, slightly north of the center of the bay's crescent, is the Pajaro Valley. This small but fertile area is bordered to the north and east by the southern tip of the Santa Cruz Mountains. The Gabilan Mountains separate the valley floor from the much larger but equally fertile Salinas Valley to the southeast and from Monterey to the south. The western edge of the valley faces the Pacific. Its unique geography and relative isolation give the Pajaro Valley an identity distinct from that of the other communities in the Monterey Bay region.

Watsonville, the most important town in the Pajaro Valley, is a small agrarian community with a distinctly Mexican character. According to the 2000 US Census, 75 percent of the town's roughly 44,000 residents are Hispanic. Entering Watsonville on Main Street from the south, one finds a small verdant plaza with a large gazebo, a fountain, and numerous benches. On most days, older Mexican men, usually retired farmworkers, congregate in the square to tell stories. Continuing north on Main Street, one passes various businesses, most of them targeting the Mexican community. Directly across from the plaza, for example, is Ritmo Latino (Latin Rhythm), a Spanish-language music store. There are also jewelers, western-style clothing stores, *taquerías* (taco stands), *panaderías* (bakeries), and numerous money-wiring services displaying their rates for money transfers to Mexico. At the northern end of Main Street, across from the Delicias Taquería, is San Patricio's (Saint Patrick's), the local Catholic Church. Watsonville feels very different from both Santa Cruz and Monterey.[7]

Demographically and economically, Watsonville resembles Salinas, to its southeast. The city of Salinas, the birthplace of novelist John Steinbeck, sits at the northern end of a valley that bears its name and is one of California's most productive agricultural regions.[8] Like Watsonville, Salinas boasts a temperate climate and fertile soil that make large-scale commercial farming highly profitable. Both Watsonville and Salinas rely on Mexican laborers to fuel their labor-intensive agriculture-based local economies.

Despite their similar economic and demographic profiles, Watsonville differs from Salinas in several significant respects—most markedly in the ways in which their agricultural industries and labor relations have developed. As in much of California, large-scale commercial agriculture with corporate absentee owners dominates the Salinas Valley. Vegetable row crops such as lettuce, broccoli, and cauliflower are grown on very large parcels of land. The area around Watsonville, however, has been mostly cultivated by local families. Strawberry farms have been the dominant agricultural employers in the area in recent years, preceded by the vegetable canneries before them. This point is important, for while organized labor has enjoyed a long presence in Salinas, as well as in Watsonville, different unions have organized different agricultural sectors in the two areas. Whereas Salinas saw massive union mobilization of its lettuce pickers by the UFW, Watsonville's extensive canneries were represented by the Teamsters.[9] UFW mobilization in Watsonville's fields has been limited historically. The last major instance of such mobilization occurred during a massive UFW strike in neighboring Salinas Valley in 1970. Thus, while both regions have been organized, demography, industry, and geography have shaped their labor organizing quite differently.

Understanding the UFW Strawberry Campaign

The tumultuous organizing history at the Coastal Berry Company between 1996 and 2003 can be explained by using a sociological framework of networks, organizations, and institutions. Networks and organizations draw from and develop norms of behavior that influence the actions of individual and collective actors. While these cultural and institutional arrangements do not determine outcomes, they do shape and constrain the range of acceptable behaviors. For individuals operating within strong networks, cultural norms and values influence behavior by providing cognitive schemas used to interpret behavior and interests. Similarly, institutional processes serve as the "rules of the game" that shape interorganizational dynamics among collective actors. Institutional norms also influence the form, strategy, and identity that organizations take.

Through these theoretical lenses, it becomes clear that the Comité beat the UFW in three elections not because of its heavy-handedness, as some have suggested, but rather because of the collective strength of individual bonds among the workers. At Coastal Berry, immigrant networks spanned vertically across the organizational structure of the company. Some immigrants held relatively high-status positions within the company's hierarchy. Because of their occupational position or office, these individuals had social power over other workers. Those in supervisory roles had authority to reassign workers to new positions, thereby influencing the subordinates' working conditions and wages. Perhaps not coincidentally, several early supporters of creating a Comité held such supervisory positions. Individuals in these positions had the most to lose from a successful unionization campaign and were active in organizing resistance to the UFW. Kin or kin-like relationships between supervisors and workers further strengthened networks enmeshed in the organization. Even when the UFW had a large number of professionally trained organizers in the fields, it lacked the pre-established ties of the Comité. What the Comité lacked in organizational structure, it made up for in its network strength, which proved quite robust in the early stages of the campaign, much to the annoyance of the UFW. These patron-client ties were the reason workers at the company declined to side with the UFW.

Social networks and interactions within them have long been an important part of the Central Coast strawberry industry and labor market. Immigrant networks comprising workers from one of a variety of different ethnic backgrounds have worked in this industry, which is dominated by relatively small landholdings. The small scale of strawberry production at peak harvest time allows for successful operations with as few as two dozen individuals. This tends to engender close and sustained contact between owners and workers, who develop bonds that extend beyond the calculus of economic exchange. These social ties mitigate traditional theoretical divisions between labor and capital.

Occupational mobility within the industry further blurs the distinction between workers and owners. Over time, individual members of successive immigrant groups have transitioned from pickers to growers. In recent decades, Mexicans have dominated the workforce. However, Mexican-origin individuals occupy positions at all levels of the industry, including that of owner. These farmers will often draw on kin and quasi-kin networks for their labor needs. The networks formed between workers and farmers on these operations can be strong. Although Mexican farmers tend to be the least capitalized farm operators, they often have the advantage of commanding strong loyalty among their workers. The same dynamic can be present at larger operations, where kin and quasi-kin networks are embedded within the organizational structure.

Coastal Berry and other firms targeted by the UFW experienced such mixes of kinship and corporate organization. Pickers at some operations were very much in favor of having their industry organized by the UFW. For them, unionization would curb the excesses of dishonest growers and foremen, regulate pay schedules, and perhaps even facilitate wage increases. Others were unsure. They worked for well-capitalized growers, made a decent living, and even enjoyed good benefits. With the money they made during nine months of hard labor in the United States, they were able to live comfortably in Mexico for the remaining three months of the year, which coincide with the long Christmas holiday season. For some union-skeptical workers, health care followed them and their families across the border.[10] The picking season was short, and time was precious. An organizing drive might disrupt their plans to make as much money as possible within the season's short time frame. At best, they were skeptical about the benefits of such a campaign. Still, the majority of workers interviewed by this researcher expressed indifference toward unionization at the beginning of the campaign. They did not know enough about either the UFW or organizing campaigns to have a strong opinion on the matter. In early spring of the 1997 growing season, organizers had not yet visited the fields.

Coastal Berry worker Eddie Hernández, who was in his mid-thirties, expressed ambivalence in the early stages of the campaign. Hernández had not been in the strawberry fields as long as some of the other workers, but he did have a good understanding of the industry and the role of Mexican workers in it. He also knew about the benefits of collective action. As a student of agro-industrial engineering at La

Universidad Autónoma del Estado de Hidalgo in Mexico, he had been involved in student movements to assist local factory workers. Along with other student groups, Eddie Hernández's organization succeeded in pressuring the Confederación Mexicana de Trabajadores (Mexican Confederation of Workers, or CMT) to demand better working conditions in factories in the state of Hidalgo. Despite his prior experience with labor movements, Hernández did not immediately join the union when he heard about the UFW campaign. In his own words, *"No los conocía muy bien y quería saber más sobre ellos* ("I didn't know them very well, and I wanted to learn more about them").

Eddie Hernández began to research the UFW, asking other farmworkers who had been in the area longer than he had about the union. He also went to the Watsonville Public Library, where, with the help of the bilingual staff, he was able to find newspaper articles and books about the union. What he learned made him uneasy. He was not convinced that UFW representation was in the best interest of workers at his company. His beliefs were further solidified when he tried to have conversations about the union and the industry with the organizers who came around the fields where he was working. Hernández claims that one organizer referred to him as an *indio pendejo* ("stupid Indian") for not wanting the union. When coworkers started talking about forming an independent workers group in the fields to counter the advances of the union, he was quick to join them in their efforts.[11]

Marina Carrasco, a fieldworker in her late thirties, saw things somewhat differently than Eddie did. At the time I interviewed her, she had been working in the Central Coast strawberry fields for almost fifteen years, with little more than a bad back to show for it. More than once, she had had to fend off sexual advances from unscrupulous foremen and supervisors. Carrasco and other women claimed that, in the fields, sexual favors could be exchanged for good jobs. Because she neither pandered to her superiors nor accepted their unwanted advances, she was consistently passed over for promotion. Younger women with half her experience were often placed in easier and better-paying jobs. This frustrated Carrasco because she was a very hard worker, and everyone knew it.

Marina Carrasco was encouraged by the prospect of a unionization campaign. She had little faith in the farmers or their managers, feeling that without a little pressure, the growers were never going to treat workers well. She had been in the fields long enough to know about the potential benefits of a unionized workforce. Strict promotion and seniority policies would curb the abuses of devious managers. A grievance policy would give workers recourse against unfair treatment.

She even thought that perhaps the wages would go up. When UFW organizers knocked on the door of her trailer in northern Santa Cruz County, she immediately agreed to support the union. Carrasco quickly became a lead organizer in her work crew. For most of the campaign, she was an outspoken and tireless organizer for the union.

Like the workers, strawberry farmers are a disparate bunch. They come from a variety of backgrounds and have broad differences of opinion. Jack Reilly, one such farmer, was not at all excited about the prospect of an organizing campaign.[12] He did not trust the UFW, concerned about what he thought would be lies and half-truths the union would spread about the industry in Los Angeles and San Francisco newspapers. Reilly thought that consumers in the cities, as well as some churches and other liberal groups, might believe it all. He deeply resented this possible outcome and took it as a personal insult when the UFW spoke of the harsh treatment and deplorable working conditions that workers suffered under local farmers, who made millions from the strawberries.

True, Reilly was very prosperous, but he liked to think that he was a generous *patrón* and citizen, and many in the community agreed.[13] He paid some of the highest wages in the industry, and health coverage at his farm extended across the border to cover both workers and their families. At the end of every season, he always had a huge *carne asada* barbecue for his workers and raffled off a variety of gifts, some of which were quite expensive. In good years, Reilly and other growers have raffled off everything from baseball caps and jackets to new pickup trucks. Reilly would often sponsor workers' soccer teams, supplying them with uniforms and equipment. He also managed his own latrine services for the fieldworkers, instead of contracting that function out to one of the numerous port-o-potty businesses in the area. His custom-built latrines with separate washing areas were well known in the industry, according to *Santa Cruz Sentinel* reporter Trina Kleist, whom I interviewed in September 2000.

Reilly's generosity extended to the community of Watsonville as well as to his workers. Although he did not actively publicize the fact, he was a significant contributor to the city, particularly its youth and sports programs. He once funded the creation of a neighborhood playground on the edge of town, adjacent to a Mexican neighborhood. When some baseball teams could not raise enough money for new uniforms, league officials knew they could rely on Reilly's quiet patronage. According to Henry Fernández, a local community leader and politician, whom I interviewed in May 2000, much of Reilly's largess has gone directly to the Mexican community. It irked Jack Reilly that farmers' contributions to the local community might be dismissed by the union in its efforts to portray the industry in a negative light.

Another prominent figure in the campaign was Elida Vasquez, a grower of Mexican descent, who has lived most of her life in the Pajaro Valley. Although she was born in Zacatecas, Mexico, her family moved to the Central Coast when she was very young. Elida has been farming in the Pajaro Valley for over thirty years. During that time, she has worked very hard and done well in a mostly white, male-dominated industry. She is well known and respected in the farming community and is the past president of a major countywide farmers' organization. While not always prosperous, she is proud and happy to be a farmer and has long-established good relationships with pickers. As she told me in October 2000: "Some workers have been with us since '77. That's twenty-two, twenty-three years, so you get to know your workforce."

As a Mexicana growing up in Pajaro Valley, Vasquez knew the UFW well. She remembers listening to UFW organizers speak at Watsonville High in the 1960s. They had spoken of self-sufficiency for Mexican immigrants, including owning gas stations and obtaining community health care. She now sees those words as empty promises: "When I was a kid at Watsonville High, I believed and we followed Cesar [Chavez]. There were big dreams and promises. Almost thirty years later, the union has not lived up to any of those promises. To be a farmer, you've got to be a farmworker, too. I care for my workers."

The UFW's latest efforts in the strawberry industry troubled her, since she did not believe that the union had accomplished much for workers in the past. As a farmer in the close-knit Pajaro Valley grower community, she wondered about the adverse economic effects of the union. When workers at her farm ignored the UFW organizers who came by her fields on a couple of occasions, she was deeply relieved. The fact that her workers were not interested in being organized by the UFW confirmed her belief that the union was "supporting farmworkers who didn't want support and weren't asking for it."

Sustained interactions among farmers and workers created behavioral norms that served as templates for everyday action. Among these were rules of conduct that stipulated mutual responsibilities and obligations for those engaged in the production process. These rules are the reason that Jack Reilly and Elida Vasquez felt that the UFW's presence in the strawberry industry was unjustified and might even be harmful. They saw themselves as good farmers, meaning that they cared about the people who worked for them, respected their contributions to the production process, and paid them well for their labor. Because of the close long-term relationships Elida Vasquez had developed with workers at her farm, she was wary of the union's overtures to them. These relationships can take on a strong historical dimension, particularly among local farmers. Both Reilly and Vasquez grew up in the Pajaro Valley amid stories and personal experiences about the UFW. For them, and farmers like them, such personal histories and norms of conduct clearly influenced their views on the union and the current campaign.

Personal histories in Mexico and the Central Coast berry fields also influenced the roles played by Eddie and other workers in these labor organization struggles. It was a serious affront to be referred to as an *indio pendejo*. Such off-color epithets, while not uncommon among intimates, are not used outside one's immediate social group without being considered highly offensive. The fact that an organizer might use these words to refer to a picker reinforced the belief among some workers that a significant social divide existed between the UFW and the majority of workers who had recently arrived from Mexico.

The UFW had been largely absent from the fields during the 1980s and early 1990s, a period of immense Mexican immigration into the American agriculture industry. Few of the campaign organizers had actual experience organizing farmworkers. According to a UFW organizing coordinator, "There were a lot of inexperienced organizers, and I think that those organizers were under some pressure to produce numbers—and it's good, they produced them, but it just wasn't real" (August 2000). This lack of organizing experience precluded the union from being fully aware of the social relations found among workers in the local industry. The same UFW organizer went on to say, "I don't think that we were ever able to correctly identify the leadership [among the workers]. Never ever, ever. I don't think even to this day we know. We knew who was in the Comité right, but beyond that I don't even think we knew who could move the [work] crew" (August 2000). Similar sentiments were expressed by other UFW personnel as well as by knowledgeable outsiders. By failing to understand the significance of social networks, the UFW was unable to account for their important influences when the union was formulating its organizing strategy. As Eddie Hernández's example demonstrates, however, these micro-level forces mattered immensely when it came to individual decision making. For workers as well as farmers, economic behavior was network-driven, not market-driven.

Networks, Organizations, and Institutions: A Theoretical Foundation

The UFW organized from above, employing a strategy that focused on employers as organizations. This approach failed to account for the power of patron-client relationships within the workforce, which doomed the union's grassroots efforts. However, that same organization-based approach can be credited for the ultimate success of the union. This book explains how this happened by taking a close look at social networks in the strawberry fields, the formal organizations involved in the campaign, and the social institutions that eventually determined the campaign's outcome. In the early stages of the campaign, the UFW was unable to overcome the power of social networks among workers in the fields. However, the union's superior organizational capabilities afforded it institutional knowledge that it used to deal effectively with the ALRB, the industry, and the wider public. Mobilization of extensive institutional processes allowed the union ultimately to secure a foothold for organized labor in the California strawberry industry. This new theoretical framework incorporating networks, organizations, and institutions is compatible with—but ultimately departs from—prior theoretical perspectives on the UFW, which have focused on internal union troubles or political climates to explain the union's difficulties organizing farmworkers.

Although the UFW faced obstacles presented by the strong preexisting social networks of workers, worker resistance to unionization did not impede the UFW from achieving numerous important successes, particularly in the early stages of the campaign. For instance, by arranging the sale of the Gargiulo Company to pro-union investors, the union managed to neutralize a potentially hostile company. It also secured the backing of prominent and influential allies in government and industry at the state and national levels, and it gained the firm support of organized labor and the American social movement sector as a whole.

The UFW then made use of its established connections to a broad range of progressive social movement organizations. In March 1998, for example, the folk music trio Peter, Paul, and Mary gave a benefit concert in nearby Santa Cruz. At a rally supporting workers' rights later that month in New York City, Gloria Steinem told a thousand people: "It's criminal…. We are here for the most basic of rights, the right to organize" (Associated Press, March 28, 1998). As in previous UFW unionization campaigns, the Catholic Church also became involved and lent its support. In June 1998, three clergy members from St. Louis (home to the Monsanto Corporation) visited local strawberry fields and wrote a critical report of the working conditions there (UFW press release, June 8, 1998). At the same time, the UFW publicized these activities as part of a skillfully orchestrated media campaign to win public support. These achievements and the UFW's strategies together look like a textbook case of political process and resource mobilization in social movements (McAdam 1982; McCarthy and Zald 1977).

This case deceptively appears straightforward when approached from a conventional social movements perspective. When they assess the feasibility of collective action, social movement scholars typically focus on factors such as political climate, potential allies, organizational form, and the availability—and strategic use—of resources. According to these criteria, the UFW should have been well positioned for victory at Coastal Berry. The union was a well-funded and highly structured organization with a meticulously conceived plan for social justice. It also enjoyed broad support from the public and private sectors. It was, after all, the union of Cesar Chavez, who had done so much to better the lot of Mexican people in the United States. From this perspective, it was almost inconceivable that workers would not be in favor of the union. It appeared that the UFW would easily succeed in its unionization efforts.

The union's successes have been a prominent source of data for the development of social movement theory. J. Craig Jenkins and Charles Perrow's (1977) well-cited article in the field is a classic example of the resource mobilization perspective. Their study examines the difference in outcomes between the National Farm Labor Union in the 1940s and the UFW in the 1960s. They attribute the success of the UFW to its ability to cultivate elite allies such as sympathetic government administrators, the Catholic Church, established labor organizations, and urban liberals.

The argument that elite allies have contributed significantly to the UFW's success has received more recent attention from Marshall Ganz, who took a leave of absence from Harvard College in 1964 to become Director of Organizing for the UFW during the 1960s. Ganz returned to Harvard after a twenty-eight-year absence to complete a PhD in sociology, with the UFW as the subject of his doctoral dissertation. Ganz (2000) argues that Jenkins and Perrow (1977) do not sufficiently explain the UFW's success with their argument that a more favorable political opportunity structure between 1965 and 1972 allowed the UFW to succeed after an earlier rival failed. According to Ganz, it was the UFW's superior "strategic capacity" that allowed it to innovate and rapidly respond to local conditions in the field, thus outmaneuvering better-funded, more established competitors. This strategic capacity and the UFW's success are rooted in the organizational structure of the union, preestablished community organizing networks, and the personal resources and resourcefulness of UFW organizers. As outsiders with resources but no local contacts, the Agricultural Workers Organizing Committee (AWOC) which was chartered by the AFL-CIO in 1959, was unable to organize workers as effectively as the UFW.

The UFW's superior strategic capacity allowed it to overcome what Ganz (borrowing a term from Stinchcombe 1965) called a "liability of newness," enabling it to outperform the older, more established AWOC between 1959 and 1966. However, in its strawberry campaign between 1996 and 2003, the UFW can be characterized as afflicted by a "liability of senescence," a term Ganz uses to describe the earlier AWOC. "Ironically," he writes, "the abundance of internal resources to which well-established groups have access may make it harder to innovate by making it easier for them to keep doing the same thing wrong" (2000: 1043). Recall that the UFW entered the strawberry industry as a well-funded, well-regarded labor union with an impressive organizational repertoire, yet it was outmaneuvered by an underfunded, loosely organized group of company workers with few resources and no political clout. Whereas in its earlier stages the UFW made effective use of strategic capacity to infiltrate worker networks, during the current campaign the union's limited local connections proved detrimental to its organizing efforts.

In understanding the rise of the Comité and the eventual success of the UFW at Coastal Berry, it is helpful to account for the behavior of individuals and organizations by understanding how the interests of individual and collective social actors, and the realization of these interests, are influenced by the rules of social exchange that dominate social relations in particular contexts.[14] Networks and formal organizations feature prominently in this approach. Cultural norms and institutional arrangements found in networks and among organizations influence the behavior of social actors while in turn being influenced by the behavior of these individual and collective actors.

Social networks are particularly salient to this case. The power of the Comité lay in the strong bonds within the networks of immigrant farmworkers. These networks underlay the failure of the UFW's grassroots efforts during the campaign. Eventually, however, the UFW's superior organizational capacity allowed it to surpass the Comité in the political, legal, and corporate aspects of the campaign. The Comité's failure to adequately formalize its organizational structure led to its demise as a farmworker union. Thus, whereas the UFW lacked the rich network-based ties that worked to the advantage of the Comité, the

Comité lacked the formal organizational structure necessary to fend off attacks from the UFW.

The concept of organizational fields helps in developing a localized and specific understanding of network and organizational interactions.[15] Extending the work of Bourdieu (1996), Weber (1978), and DiMaggio (1985), Neil Fligstein uses the concept of fields to explain how social actions occur within a given social space. According to Fligstein, "Fields contain collective actors who try to produce a system of domination in that space. To do so requires the production of a local culture that defines local social relations between actors" (2001: 15). Sustained interactions among a broad range of collective actors give rise to behavioral norms that regulate the conduct of organizations within these fields.

This perspective is applicable to a broader range of situations than Fligstein's discussion of firms operating within markets. According to Fligstein, collective actors seek to create stability and reduce uncertainty by creating rules that govern behavior within fields, or organizational domains. However, firms are not always capable of producing such rules, or *governance structures* as Fligstein calls them, so they must rely on the state to implement the laws and policies that structure interfirm interactions. It should be noted that stability within markets is a relative concept. Any field consists of incumbents and challengers vying for influence or control of state apparatuses. The governance structures simply provide the "rules of the game." Fligstein writes, "The shape of initial regulatory institutions has a profound effect on subsequent capitalist development. They define the current state of rules and what is permissible" (2001: 40). Once these rules are in place, they provide a context that structures later interactions among firms in the field. The ALRA is an example of an institution; it regulates the behavior of employers and employees in the California agriculture industry. As a key organizational actor in the establishment of the ALRA in 1975, the UFW had a long history with the institution. The Comité did not share this familiarity.

Fligstein's model suggests that effective participation in an organizational field and the ability to influence the local balance of power require the use of social organizational vehicles with knowledge of and ability to manipulate institutional processes that have been implemented to constrain and enable collective actors. This phenomenon can be seen in the California agriculture industry, which has developed models of industrial organization conducive to rapid economic development facilitated by favorable relations with the state apparatus. More recently, the UFW achieved success and prominence as it too assumed a formal bureaucratized organizational structure and adopted strategies well suited for the institutionalized relationships that had developed between the market economy and the liberal democratic political system of the United States.

The Comité was not an effective organizational vehicle because it possessed only a minimal organizational capacity for effectively understanding and manipulating the institutional procedures set in place to mediate disputes between labor and the industry. Rather, the Comité is best understood as a network attempting to formally organize. The necessity of a bureaucratic form to operate successfully within an organizational field explains the failure of the Comité as a farm labor union. It was unable to develop the organizational infrastructure necessary to compete in the legal-political arena. Its lack of formal bureaucratic organization also explains why the group was unable to effectively conduct the day-to-day operations required of a collective bargaining agent, which led to its 2002 loss against the UFW. This organizational perspective cannot, however, account for the group's initial popularity, nor does it explain how the workers' committee was able to outmaneuver the UFW in the fields but not in the office or courtroom. To answer these two questions, one must consider culture and institutions.

Cultural forces influenced the trajectory of the organizing campaign on two levels: that of the individual operating within networks and that of the organization in terms of institutions that determine possible interactions among collective actors. This account of cultural influences on social behavior draws heavily from Ann Swidler's concept of culture as a source of strategies for social action. Strategy refers here not to conscious plans to obtain specific goals but rather more generally to a means of organizing behavior to obtain multiple goals. Swidler presents culture as "a 'toolkit' of symbols, stories, rituals, and word-views, which people may use in varying configurations to solve different kinds of problems" (1986: 273). Swidler's conceptualization of culture diverges from the Weberian approach, in which culture shapes action by providing ultimate ends that guide behavior. Swidler writes, "Action is not determined by one's values; rather action and values are organized to take advantage of cultural competencies" (1986: 275). Thus, culture provides actors with templates of possible actions. Thinking about culture this way helps to explain why some individuals in the strawberry fields may not have wanted UFW representation even though they were willing to concede the benefits of unionization.

Cultural strategies do not represent a unified system oriented in a specific direction; directions taken can be diverse and conflicting, creating a broad range of possible adaptations. At the individual level this breadth of utility helps to explain why some workers may have been very much in favor of the UFW while others were more hesitant about unionization. For collective actors, the adaptation of certain procedural norms and a repertoire of strategies signify the institutional work of organizations. Organizational capacity implies a set of cultural competencies that organizations use to navigate their particular organizational fields. Whereas the UFW exhibited a high degree of competency in its interactions with other formal organizations, the Comité did not. Reviewing a wide range of materials related to the UFW campaign reveals how personal networks constrained and enabled the economic behavior of individuals by providing templates of acceptable behavior. Similar norms of conduct determine interorganizational behavior. By paying attention to networks, organizations, and institutions, we can better understand the outcome of the UFW campaign.

---

[1]Growers will "disk," plow under, a crop when it is not economically feasible to harvest. While doing so usually entails considerable financial loss, it is sometimes more cost-effective than harvesting the produce for market. In this particular case, the UFW and many farmworkers thought the growers were acting out of spite and not financial concern. However, according to a story circulating around the grower community at the time, the owners disked the fields for economic reasons. Because of the strike, the fruit was not picked in time and was thus rendered unmarketable. This version of events further asserts that quarreling among business partners also led to the dissolution of the farm.

[2]The event received coverage in all major dailies in California and most of the country. The *Los Angeles Times*, the *New York Times*, and the *Washington Post* all ran articles on the march. The left-leaning Mexican daily *La Jornada* ran two stories on the campaign immediately after the march. Unconfirmed reports state that a Japanese media team was present as well.

[3] Although the AFL-CIO was by far the largest donor of material and human resources, it is important to note that other organizations, such as the National Farm Worker Ministry, also contributed significant staff to the campaign.

[4]Davis and the California State Assembly were labor-friendly during his tenure as governor from 1999 to 2003.

[5]The most detailed version of these events is found in three articles by Marc Lifsher: "How Monsanto and Democrats failed in efforts to aid UFW," *Wall Street Journal*, August 5 1998, p. CA1; "ALRB shuffle stalls hearing on union vote," *Wall Street Journal*, January 27, 1999, p. CA1; and "Confidential memo suggests Coastal Berry favored UFW," *Wall Street Journal*, October 13, 1999, p. CA1.

[6] Although the English word *consultant* is formally translated as *consultor* in Spanish, I most often heard the Spanglish *consultante* from workers in reference to anti-UFW consultants.

[7]Santa Cruz is an affluent college town and popular summer resort. It is liberal-minded and progressive in its politics. Its largely white population is sometimes thought by Watsonville residents to have a greater environmental than social conscience. Monterey is patrician and sedate; it is even more white and affluent than Santa Cruz. The influence of 1960s youth counterculture that pervades Santa Cruz is conspicuously absent here.

[8]The other two regions are the central San Joaquin Valley, to the east of Salinas, and the Coachella Valley, southeast of Los Angeles.

[9]Between 1967 and 1977, the Teamsters and the UFW brokered a series of pacts designed to settle jurisdictional disputes. While not always followed, those agreements generally kept the Teamsters in the packing sheds and canneries, and the UFW in the fields. Monterey Mushrooms, Inc., represents an example of where the pact has not always been followed. The UFW has represented workers there on and off since 1979. Other Watsonville-area growers that have had UFW representation include West Coast Farms and Sakata Ranch, Inc. West Coast Farms is no longer in operation, and Sakata no longer has a UFW contract.

[10]Some of the better insurance plans covered workers in Mexico as well as the United States and were highly valued.

[11]Eddie Hernández is thoughtful and knowledgeable about the world around him. During the 2000 presidential campaign, we watched George W. Bush's half-Mexican nephew being interviewed in Spanish by Jorge Ramos, a widely known Latin American newscaster. Hernández noted what he took to be the transparency of Bush's Spanish-speaking strategy to gain the Hispanic vote. He was quick to add, however, referring to the efforts of his anti-UFW Comité, "At the state level, a Republican governor helps our case more than a Democrat."

[12]Jack Reilly is the only individual discussed here whom I did not interview. The information in this profile comes from conversations with various friends of his, his secretary, and newspaper articles in which he has been featured.

[13]Reilly's reputation was acknowledged by the community leaders and pickers whom I interviewed.

[14] This perspective is grounded in the field of economic sociology. See Dobbin (2004); Smelser and Swedberg (2005); and Swedberg (2003) for a theoretical overview.

[15] Minkoff and McCarthy (2005) suggest this approach to scholars looking to reintegrate organizational analysis into the study of social movements.

3

The Strawberry Industry Campaign

This chapter introduces labor and capital exchanges in the California agriculture industry and chronicles events in the Central Coast strawberry industry during the UFW unionization campaign. Understanding the events surrounding the organizing campaign requires some background about California agriculture. In the first section I introduce a conceptual framework that helps explain the development of a modern industry and the historic interactions between dominant organizational actors. The framework is followed by a detailed description of the unionization drive in the strawberry industry from 1995 to 2000 with a focus on the Coastal Berry Company, where the UFW concentrated its efforts from 1997 to 2000. The UFW organizing campaign was originally intended to be an industry-wide effort, with particular focus on the cooler-shippers that dominated the industry. The campaign launched very publicly with numerous grower, pro-labor, civic, and political groups involved. Unionization efforts eventually focused on Coastal Berry, the largest strawberry producer in the state, which had just been sold to union-friendly investors. From the summer of 1998, when the Comité filed an election request with the ALRB, the fight moved from the fields into the courtroom, where the matter of unionization would finally be settled in late 2000.

The Political Economy of Agriculture

The agrarian context of the union mobilization drive, a central aspect of this study, is addressed by the significant body of literature on the political economy of agriculture. These studies explore various aspects of agricultural systems in advanced industrial societies. Important themes in the literature include markets, labor, and the relationship between the state, agricultural producers, and labor. These concepts are essential for understanding the UFW campaign.

The concepts stated above are studied in the field of political economy of agriculture, which examines agrarian relations of production and the socio-political contexts in which these processes occur.[1] The field focuses on the commercial production of agricultural products in industrialized settings that employ corporate models of organization. Like their urban counterparts, agro-industrial production systems can be characterized by the pursuit of profit maximization and the use of rationalized production processes. Commercial agriculture is also similar to urban industrial production in that it is subject to state regulation. Legislation on subsidies, tariffs, trade agreements, immigration, and labor is especially important for the industry. Other aspects of agricultural production including product quality, workplace safety, environmental conditions, and labor relations are also influenced by government policy.

The extensive role of the state in commercial agricultural production has prompted various interest groups to vie for state favor (Clemens 1997; Hansen 1991; Browne 1988). Industry lobby groups include farm bureaus, growers associations, and specific commodity trade groups. Labor unions and community-based organizations represent the interests of labor in the industry. Various groups within the state also figure prominently in the commercial agricultural production process. Most of these, such as the California Occupational Safety and Health Administration (OSHA) and the Agricultural Labor Relations Board (ALRB), are regulatory bodies. The agriculture industry also benefits from state extension programs that research and develop technological and scientific innovations advantageous to the industry. The dynamic interactions between the various state, industry, and civic advocacy groups in this arena constitute the commercial agricultural production complex.

Each organization within this complex is governed by a set of values and interests. Sometimes these values and interests overlap, as in the case of the farm bureau and the growers associations. At other times, groups such as farm labor organizations and growers have divergent interests. Historically, the state has assisted the industry in its endeavors. In the last three decades of the twentieth century, however, the role of the state and all its various agencies has been transformed to that of mediator between the various interests in the agricultural production complex (Majka 1982). Two examples include the California Department of Pesticide Regulations and the ALRB. The various extension programs whose aims are more narrowly scientific and technological form an exception to this rule. Whether regulatory or research oriented, government practices weigh heavily on growers and workers alike.

State legislation and the openness of political administrations have been critical to the success of farmworker organizations since the 1960s. The state has the unique role of negotiating between capital interests and labor concerns. As mediator, the state has the power to significantly alter the balance of power between labor and capital in the agriculture sector by favoring one group over the other. For example, state legislation can make organizing more or less difficult for labor unions depending on the stringency of conditions that must be met to achieve union recognition. Throughout most of their history, farm labor movements have been significantly hindered by their inability to influence government policy or legislation. As a result, for much of California history, state intervention has favored grower interests.

The arrangement among workers, growers, and the state began to change in the late 1960s as organized labor began to assert itself in the agriculture industry. The establishment in 1975 of an agricultural labor relations board to oversee labor disputes completely changed the dynamic between the state, growers, and labor in California. No longer would growers' interests consistently dominate the agriculture production complex. Moreover, and most importantly, the state could no longer be as partisan as it had been in the past regarding matters of labor and industry. The Agricultural Labor Relations Act established a legal framework that was to serve as a basis from which to adjudicate any disputes between workers and growers. It forced the state to mediate to a far greater extent than it had in the past.

The rise of organized labor has also forced the state to assume a greater regulatory role in the agriculture industry. Farm labor unions have had success publicizing the harmful effects of pesticides and other chemicals used in agricultural production. Growers face far greater scrutiny of their use of pesticides as a result of this awareness. This scrutiny is often seen as an inconvenience to growers, who resent the subsequent state regulations as an encroachment upon their farming practices. To further the ire of the grower community, organized labor has also succeeded in having some pesticides banned, which has serious implications for American growers, who are forced to compete in a global market against producers in other countries who do not face similar restrictions. Besides regulating the use of pesticides, state agencies such as the California Division of Occupational Safety and Health (Cal OSHA) mandate that working conditions meet state code, which requires that workers are given adequate breaks for meals and rest, and have access to drinking water and clean restroom facilities. These are contentious issues in the fields as labor groups demand compliance with state regulations for workers. Some farmers that I interviewed claimed that theirs is one of the most highly scrutinized workplaces in the economy.

Not all government agencies irk the grower community. Indeed, the United States has a long history of assisting farmers in various ways. Some programs at the state and federal level are highly beneficial and often vital to the success and competitiveness of commercial agriculture. For example, fruit and vegetable producers receive water subsidies, and tariffs on imports protect domestic producers. Finally, growers enjoy certain tax incentives that other sectors of the economy do not receive. Government programs also provide assistance with the production process through state agricultural extension offices that serve a variety of needs for the grower community. One of the most important is the research and development of new techniques and procedures to make farming more productive and thus more profitable. Recently, genetic research into crops has proven valuable to farmers. For example, the development of drought-resistant corn or berries that grow in sandy soil can be useful to producers. Agricultural extension program officers also work in other arenas of production—such as pest control, irrigation, and the testing of equipment that increases the efficiency of farming.

A political economy of agriculture perspective helps explain interactions between capitalist enterprises and the state in agrarian environments. Such a perspective is useful given the long history of grower involvement in California's political system. I now discuss the central role of labor in agriculture and explain how the industry has conspired with the state to ensure a dependable supply of low-wage, unorganized workers.

The Role of Labor in Agriculture

As revenue-generating enterprises, growers are driven by profit maximization. To this end, they employ strategies of capitalistic production to increase the income potential of their firms. For example, growers have been successful in applying technological and scientific innovation to the realm of production to reduce production costs and maximize profit (Stoll 1998). Labor costs are high for fruit, vegetable, and tree crops. Depending on the crop, labor can range between 30 percent and 60 percent of the total production costs in a season. This is why, where possible, growers have thus invested heavily in mechanization to reduce the cost of labor (Friedland, Barton, and

Thomas 1981). Cotton production is one example in which mechanization has proven profitable. Other sectors of the industry, such as garlic, onions, and strawberries, have had more difficulty with mechanization. Reducing labor costs may not be easy, but when possible the benefits to growers are high.

Labor maintains a central role in agricultural production. Commercial agriculture demands a regular labor force willing to work at irregular intervals over the course of a growing season. To ensure that these peculiar demands are met, the grower community works closely with state and federal agencies. Without a facilitating state to ensure a constant and overabundant pool of labor, large-scale commercial agriculture in California and indeed in the United States would not be possible.[2] From the late nineteenth century to the present, agricultural producers have managed to get legislation enacted that secures a cheap and readily available labor force (Calavita 1992; Majka 1980). State legislation in the form of labor and immigration policies has provided major benefits to commercial agriculture. This type of legislation often has been in the form of favorable or restrictive immigration policies that target specific minority or ethnic groups working in agriculture (Takaki 1989).

Until the 1970s, a long series of labor and immigration laws designed to maintain a dependable, docile, and steady workforce epitomized the approach of the state toward the agriculture industry's labor needs. Soon after statehood, legislation was designed to ensure that Asians—first Chinese and then Japanese—would be available to work California's fields (Taylor Martin and Fix 1997; Chan 1986). After the Chinese Exclusion Act of 1888, Japanese slowly became the dominant labor force in California agriculture. Japanese prosperity, however, led to a "gentleman's agreement" between the United States and Japan, which barred further Japanese immigration to the country (Guerin Gonzales 1994). The Alien Land Law, passed in 1913, excluded the foreign-born from land ownership and further hindered Asians in agriculture. Later, the state responded to xenophobic fears with the Federal Immigrant Act of 1917, which specifically targeted immigrants from Asian countries. Immigration legislation restricting Asian groups allowed for the emergence of Mexican laborers as the main workforce in Western agriculture.

Mexican workers have since dominated the West's agricultural labor market. This economic exchange is facilitated by geography as well as politics. Mexico's proximity to the United States made it more attractive as a labor pool than previous countries that had supplied the Western labor markets. The economic growth of the Southwestern states required a growing labor force; employers looked to Mexico for workers. Although illegal, American labor recruiters would often travel to the Mexican interior to entice workers to the north (Sánchez 1993). Wages in the US were much better than the average of 12 cents per day paid for farm work in the Mexican interior. In the 1920s, a railroad or agricultural worker in the United States could earn between $1 and $2 per day (Sánchez 1993). Not only were workers being pulled by the expanding economy in the north; they were also being pushed by domestic policies in Mexico. The early twentieth century was a period of social change and upheaval in Mexico. During his tenure from 1876 to 1910, the dictator Porfirio Díaz sought to modernize Mexico with American-financed railroads and the consolidation of peasant landholdings for commercial agriculture. Mexico's rail network increased thirty-fold during Díaz's 35 years in office, from 663 kilometers in 1875 to 19,748 kilometers in 1910 (Sánchez 1993). These railways were oriented in a general north-south direction, making it much easier for labor and commerce to move northward to the American cities of Tucson, El Paso, and San Antonio. During this same period the Mexican population was growing rapidly. Between 1877 and 1910, the Mexican population increased from 9.4 million to 15.2 million people (Guerin Gonzales 1994). Changes in land tenure policy meant that this burgeoning population had nearly 30 percent less arable land available for farming by the end of the Díaz regime (Guerin Gonzales 1994). The attraction of the north was clear. Between 1900 and 1930, approximately 1.5 million Mexicans migrated to the United States. This figure represents about a 10 percent loss of Mexico's population by the end of the 1920s (Sánchez 1993).

As with Asian immigrants, federal policy in the form of immigration legislation has specifically targeted Mexican immigrants destined for the American labor market. At the start of World War II, the agriculture industry in California seized the political opportunity that came from potential labor shortages and called for the state-sponsored and state-administered importation of thousands of field workers from Mexico. Grower representatives argued for the urgent creation of a stable and compliant labor force during what was called a time of national crisis. Lacking political representation, domestic farmworkers were unable to submit opposing arguments to the legislation. Capitulating to grower demands, Congress enacted the Bracero Program in 1940. After the war, growers succeeded in their efforts to have the program extended. In 1956, at the height of the Bracero Program, close to half a million workers were contracted to work in the United States. Before it was finally terminated in 1964, over 4 million Mexican laborers had been temporarily imported into the country (Edid 1994: 32). Without the direct involvement of the US government in terms of logistical infrastructure and enforcement, the program would never have enjoyed its success or longevity (Calavita 1992). Neither permanent nor American, *braceros* were not subject to American pay scales or labor conditions. They were an unusually malleable group, unorganized, and above all an extremely profitable workforce for American growers. It is no coincidence that the first successful attempt to organize farmworkers occurred in 1965, a year after Congress repealed the Bracero Program with Public Law 78 in 1964.

Immigration legislation continues to be politically contentious and economically significant. In fact, the state's task of dealing with opposing goals around issues of labor and immigration has become more complicated since the 1970s. In 1975 farmworkers succeeded in having the California Agricultural Labor Relations Act passed. This highly consequential legislation initially facilitated the efforts of farmworkers to organize.[3] It has also forced the state to arbitrate farmer-worker disputes through the California Agricultural Labor Relations Board (ALRB). Throughout the 1970s and 1980s, unauthorized immigration to the United States increased precipitously (Calavita 1992). In response, the Immigration Reform Act of 1986 (IRCA) gave legal status to 1.1 million Mexican agricultural workers and over 4 million Mexican laborers in general (Taylor, Martin, and Fix 1997; Calavita 1992). Besides providing amnesty, this act also made it illegal, for the first time in history, for employers to knowingly hire illegal workers. Sanctions, however, were largely symbolic, and employers continued to hire workers without regard to their legal status.

Later, during the 1990s, in reaction to growing anti-immigrant sentiment, the Clinton administration oversaw the expansion of the Immigration and Naturalization Service (INS) with thousands of new border guards and the implementation of increasingly sophisticated surveillance equipment attempting to stem the tide of illegal immigration. These policies and legislative initiatives, however, do not represent a coherent program to regulate immigration and the low-wage labor market but rather demonstrate an ad hoc effort to mediate between competing voices on the subject in American society (Gutiérrez 1995; Calavita 1992). In the latest phase, as recently as 2000, Mexican President Vicente Fox discussed another possible amnesty with a receptive President George W. Bush, though the events of September 11, 2001, stalled the discussions. Despite this interruption, issues of immigration and labor, particularly as they pertain to the agriculture industry, continue to play an important role in American politics and economics.

From the late 1990s and to the present, nearly all berry fieldworkers are of Mexican descent. An overwhelming majority of pickers are born in Mexico, although there is a small contingent of workers (perhaps as high as 20 percent) who were born in the United States. These Mexican Americans also tend to be disproportionately found in supervisory roles and skilled positions, such as truck drivers and loaders, relative to recently arrived Mexican immigrants.[4] Most Mexican-born workers come from the central states of Michoacán and Jalisco, although since the 1980s the proportion of indigenous people from Southern Mexico and Central America has been increasing. Men comprise 60 to 70 percent of the workforce and women 30 to 40 percent. Punchers tend to be women.[5] Although it is difficult to gauge, most observers believe that between 75 and 90 percent of workers do not have proper immigration documentation.[6] This was the workforce that experienced the campaign that is the subject of this book.

The Strawberry Campaign in Detail

Labor strife in the local strawberry industry began at VCNM Farms in Salinas in 1995. In August of that year workers discouraged with working conditions and pay rates walked off the fields. Later that same year in a state-supervised election, workers voted 332 to 50 in favor of UFW representation. Refusing to recognize the outcome of the election, VCNM's owners declared bankruptcy and plowed under their fields five days after the election (Bacon 1998).[7] For the next five years anti-union voices would use VCNM Farms as a warning: workers who chose to unionize risked losing their jobs. For the union and its supporters, the incident at VCNM underscored the necessity of a protracted, industry-wide campaign, as well as the necessity of grower neutrality. According to UFW negotiator Jorge Rivera, "We can't target one grower at a time. If we go after everyone at once, they can't do that [plow their fields.] If we strike the whole industry, they're not going to pull us down" (Barnett 1996).

The following year, the UFW, with the enthusiastic support of the AFL-CIO, decided to initiate an industry-wide campaign to organize strawberry workers. In November 1996, John Sweeney, recently elected president of the AFL-CIO, launched the National Strawberry Commission for Workers Rights, which was to coordinate the activities of the strawberry campaign around the country and forge coalitions with various civic, environmental, and religious groups (Bacon 1997). Soon after, in May 1996, the union filed 33 notices to take access and 21 notices to organize among various farms in the Central Coast region.[8] UFW and AFL-CIO organizers converged on the Central Coast fields following the announcements. Besides providing salaries for some 40 organizers, the AFL-CIO also mobilized its local labor councils around the country. The Santa Cruz chapter would later come to represent more than 80 community organizations and individuals (UFW 1998a). In November 1996, the UFW published an extensive report titled "Five Cents for Fairness: The Case for Change in the Strawberry Fields." The position paper detailed the prosperity of the strawberry industry while condemning the deplorable working conditions and poverty-level wages of the workers in the fields. According to the report, a five-cent increase in each pint of strawberries sold would significantly raise worker wages.

The union's efforts to organize the industry were almost immediately met with resistance from workers and growers alike. Local workers accused the UFW of harassment and patronizing organizing tactics. According to Sergio Mendoza, a worker at Well-Pict Inc., "They say we pick fruit with dirty hands, hands that are covered with sores and with pus, and it's not true. They say the fruit is poisoned with pesticides but we eat it every day" (Barnett and Garcia 1996). Other workers claimed that a union would be of little benefit to them. Adolfo Gasca, a worker at a well-financed Driscoll's operation, earned an average of $8 an hour and had health insurance as well as other benefits. He said, "What can the union offer me that I don't already have? They say they want to help our suffering, but I don't believe it. With every kind of work there is suffering" (ibid).

A month after the UFW report was published, the Strawberry Workers and Farmers Alliance (SWFA), a pro-industry group, accused the UFW of misleading the public with its Five Cents for Fairness campaign. According to Gary Caloroso, spokesperson for the alliance, the UFW was setting the stage for a national boycott. He countered the report, saying, "The five cent thing is a sham. They're expecting everybody to pass it on. But anytime there's a profit, everybody has their fingers in the cookie jar." He went on to say, "We're against any threats to market strawberries. We're against boycotts and we think they're laying the foundation for a national campaign to bash the industry" (Sotero 1996). Such resistance was not surprising to the UFW. Rodriguez himself acknowledged at the beginning of the campaign that it would be a "dogfight." AFL-CIO strawberry campaign coordinator Arturo Mendoza took a more pragmatic approach, saying, "It's a $700 million industry—you would expect that they'd run a good campaign" (Barnett and Garcia 1996).

The UFW was prepared for an extensive fight. The union opened its second season of organizing with a huge march for workers' rights in downtown Watsonville. Organized labor as well as other civic, religious, and environmental groups were present in solidarity with local strawberry workers. As many as 30,000 people marched down the streets of Watsonville demanding change in the industry. Later that summer, Gargiulo Company, the largest strawberry producer in the region, was sold to Maryland investors David Gladstone and Landon Butler, who renamed the company Coastal Berry. The new owners pledged neutrality in the unionization drive, ending more than a year of hostility between the UFW and Gargiulo. The UFW was pleased with the outcome of the transaction. According to Arturo Mendoza, "For the first time since we began the campaign, workers will have the opportunity to make decisions without having to look over their shoulders about what the company is thinking, or threats, or reprisals" (Baldwin Hick and Steyer 1997). Soon after the sale, the UFW announced a settlement with the company in which Gargiulo, now renamed Coastal Berry, agreed to pay $575,000 in back pay to workers it had forced to work without wages before their shifts began. Having contained the threat of the largest strawberry producer in the region, the union was now poised to take on the entire industry. In August of 1997 a class action suit similar to that filed against Gargiulo was filed against Reiter Berry Farms. With the help of the UFW, three raspberry pickers filed a class action suit on behalf of hundreds of workers against Reiter for not paying workers overtime as required by law. The suit demanded back pay to 1993 for 360 pickers, totaling $750,000 (Wilson 1997).

Also in August of 1997 the Agricultural Workers Committee (AWC) held a march through the streets of Watsonville in which several thousand farmworkers denounced the UFW. Commenting on the march, Antonio Perez, spokesperson for the so-called March for Truth, said, "This was truly a grassroots demonstration. These people were not professional organizers or union members shipped in from across the country. The people who were marching in the streets today are the people who pick the fruit you see in your stores. They are the only people who truly know what goes on in the fields every day" (Merrill 1997). The UFW dismissed the AWC, claiming the organization was a "front group" for the strawberry industry. According to Arturo Rodriguez, "They created the Agricultural Workers Committee to destroy farm workers trying to organize" (Linneman 1997). The UFW filed suits with the ALRB, arguing that growers Ed Kelly, Clint Miller, Miguel Ramos, and Jim Dutra had encouraged and coerced workers to attend the march. On August 20, the UFW filed a motion with the Santa

Cruz County superior court to prohibit the AWC from deceiving the public and to make their ties to growers known (Rodebaugh 1997).

That same day in August 1997, the UFW held a rally outside Driscoll Strawberry Associates, demanding that the cooperative honor its public statements regarding its position of neutrality toward worker unionization. The Driscoll cooperative controlled fields employing about 5,000 workers, about one-quarter of the state's pickers. According to the UFW, Driscoll claimed to be neutral regarding unionization when in fact it refused to address worker complaints of inadequate wages and health benefits or sexual harassment and failed to comply with laws regarding workplace safety. Clint Miller, a Driscoll grower distressed by the negative publicity, claimed the UFW was out to "rule or ruin" the industry. He said, "They're trying to force all of us to sign an agreement with them or they'll put us out of business. It's almost the end of the season and they haven't been able to drum up an election; it's quite obvious the workers are not interested in being controlled by the UFW and their hierarchy" (Barnett 1997). Miller was right about one thing. The second growing season of the campaign came to a close without a single election being called in the industry.

If the union was having difficulties in the fields, it was achieving notable successes in other arenas. In September 1997, Safeway, the second-largest food retailer in the country, agreed to honor workers' rights to organize. According to the UFW, 5,337 retail food stores in the country's eight largest markets, or 65 percent, had signed a pledge to support strawberry pickers (DeBare 1997). However, the impact of the agreement was unclear since no strawberries would be removed from the stores. In this respect the gesture was largely symbolic. Still, securing such a pledge from Safeway was a significant accomplishment for the UFW. The union and the supermarket chain had been bitter adversaries for years. In the 1960s and 1970s, the UFW and its supporters had boycotted Safeway stores for selling nonunion grapes. The pledge from Safeway marked a new direction in the relationship between the union and corporate entities.

The third year of the campaign opened with a series of legal battles. In early January 1998, the UFW filed a second suit against AWC seeking attorney's fees after the latter tried unsuccessfully to block the union's original suit. San Francisco attorneys Stephen P. Berzon, Mary Lynne Werlwas, and Christopher Pederson, along with UFW attorneys Marcos Camacho and Anabelle G. Cortez, asked a court to grant them $36,069 in legal fees from the group. A spokesperson for the AWC claimed the group did not have that amount of money in its coffers. The previous year, in August 1997, the UFW filed a SLAPP (Strategic

Lawsuit against Public Participation) motion against the AWC, claiming the group was misrepresenting itself and raising money fraudulently. The motion filed by the union against the AWC and another group, the Agricultural Workers Association (AWA), claimed that the two groups were not in fact independent workers' associations but rather sham groups financed and controlled by growers. In January 1998, a Santa Cruz superior court judge ruled that the union's lawsuit could move forward and awarded the UFW $8,000 in legal fees.

On another front in the campaign, the folk music group Peter, Paul, and Mary performed a benefit concert for the UFW in Santa Cruz on March 19, 1998. Later that month, in New York City, more than 1,000 people marched in solidarity for workers' rights to organize. Social commentator Gloria Steinem spoke about the conditions of strawberry workers in California and urged participants to pledge their support for the workers. Several months later, another pledge of public support for the strawberry campaign emerged: in mid-June, Salinas followed Santa Cruz to become the second major city on the Central Coast to adopt a resolution recognizing the right of workers to organize. In a 4-2 vote, the Salinas city council voted to "recognize the right of strawberry workers to organize for a better life." In addition, the city council measure also supported the local chapter of the AFL-CIO's National Strawberry Commission for Workers' Rights (UFW 1998b).

That same month, the Western Growers Association (WGA) sued the UFW and the Coastal Berry Company for illegally conspiring to unionize workers. The suit was filed in the Santa Cruz County superior court. In the suit, the WGA alleged that Coastal Berry owners had engaged in unfair labor practices by publicly stating the company's neutrality while sending letters to workers expressing their support of the union. According to Terrence R. O'Connor, an attorney for Western Legal Associates, "We want [owner David] Gladstone and Coastal Berry to stop claiming they are neutral and admit that their labor relations are handled by the UFW" (Rubenstein 1998).[9] The WGA suit further claimed that Coastal Berry had not actually been sold by Monsanto but that the transaction was part of an elaborate scheme between the alleged buyers, the union, and the Monsanto Corporation (Rubenstein 1998). An administrative law judge later dismissed the suit.

Workers at Coastal Berry also were frustrated by what they took to be the intimate relationship between the company's new owners and the UFW. As the 1998 season progressed, hostilities increased in the fields and in the courts. On July 1, an anti-UFW demonstration and work stoppage by Coastal Berry workers led to violence in the company's strawberry fields. That morning, several hundred workers gathered outside Coastal Berry's Beach Street facility in Watsonville's industrial sector. Workers upset by what they took to be a pro-union stance on the part of the company's owners blocked traffic to and from the strawberry cooler and shut down operations. The group's leaders, Sergio Leal and Jose Guadalupe Fernández, among others, presented Coastal Berry President David R. Smith with a list of demands they wanted met. Workers insisted that Smith stop interfering in matters of unionization, respect workers' rights to oppose the union, and keep in place the raise implemented by recently departed president Larry Galper. Workers insisted that Smith sign a notarized letter agreeing to these conditions.[10]

The work stoppage at Coastal Berry's main center of operations in Watsonville ended shortly after Smith signed the notarized statement agreeing to workers' demands. However, many of the protestors at the cooler decided to drive to the company's Silliman Ranch facility, where pro-union workers had refused to support the work stoppage and demonstration. Anti-UFW workers aggressively tried to force pro-union workers to stop picking berries. In the exchanges that ensued, violence broke out between the opposing groups. Three people—two women and one man—who had refused to stop picking strawberries were injured in the melee. Another man, anti-UFW leader Jose Guadalupe Fernández, was arrested. When police officers from the sheriff's department, highway patrol, and other agencies arrived on the scene of the scuffle, they were met with resistance from workers, who threw dirt clods, rocks, and wooden pallets at the officers. According to police accounts, Jose Guadalupe Fernández was instigating the crowd and obstructed traffic by extending a length of pipe across an access road. After failing to subdue Fernández with pepper spray, three law enforcement officials tackled and restrained him. The UFW would later demand the dismissal of several anti-UFW workers at Coastal Berry on the grounds that they had incited violence against pro-UFW workers. Six months later, in January 1998 and February 1999, some of these workers were dismissed from their positions at Coastal Berry. The workers later filed suits against the company, claiming that their anti-union activities were protected under the law. An ALRB ruling later found in their favor.

Worker grumblings about what they perceived to be harassment from UFW organizers coalesced into the Coastal Berry Farm Workers Committee (El Comité) in the summer of 1998. The original members of the group were better-paid workers such as truck drivers, although there was strong support among rank-and-file pickers in some crews as well. There was a mix of recent immigrants as well as workers who had been in the United States for much longer. A few were even US citizens. The Comité did not aspire to be a union in the conventional sense of the term since its principle objective was to expel the UFW from the Coastal Berry strawberry fields. Many felt that the UFW was pestering them, and that the union did not respect their wishes not to be unionized. These anti-UFW workers took their frustrations against the union and the company to the state labor board. On July 18, 1998, the Comité submitted to the Salinas office of the ALRB a petition for a representative election. After ensuring that the petition included valid signatures from at least 50.1 percent of Coastal Berry's employees, the ALRB decided to hold the election on July 23. According to the Agricultural Labor Relations Act, farm labor elections must take place within seven days of the day a petition is submitted. The UFW moved quickly to counter the efforts of the Comité.

The UFW filed with the ALRB unfair labor practice objections against the Comité and Coastal Berry. The union demanded an investigation into alleged coercion and harassment on the part of the company and the Comité in the period preceding the submission of the petition. The UFW also called for the election to be cancelled. At a California Labor Conference in Oakland attended by Senator Barbara Boxer and gubernatorial candidate Gray Davis, Arturo Rodriguez was quoted as saying, "A free election can't take place under these conditions. This scheme to stage an election at Coastal Berry ... makes a mockery of the law whose purpose is to encourage and protect the right of farm workers to organize" (Rodebaugh 1998). He also accused Coastal Berry of not disciplining foremen and tolerating abuses against the union. According to Rodriguez, "Coastal Berry has gone from promising neutrality to promoting terrorism." Rodriguez continued by saying that the Comité "is a grower group calling itself a union" (Brazil 1998). The UFW pointed to video footage of the July 1 altercation to substantiate its claims that anti-UFW workers at the company had used intimidation and violence to coerce workers into signing the petition for an election. Speaking in favor of the group, Jose Guadalupe Fernández said, "The committee started because people didn't want the union, so we didn't have any alternative. I'm about 80 percent sure that we're going to win the election. If [the workers] want to vote for us they will, and the truth will come out. I don't know what [the UFW] is afraid of" (Pacini 1998). Over the vociferous protests of the UFW, the board decided that the petition represented the valid signatures of over 50 percent of the Coastal Berry workforce and decided to proceed with the election to be held Thursday, July 23.

The ALRB-monitored election polled about 1,000 Coastal Berry workers in Santa Cruz, Monterey, and Ventura counties of California. Workers had an opportunity to cast a ballot for the Coastal Berry Farm

Workers Committee or "no union" since the UFW had not tried to get on the ballot after the Comité filed its petition. According to the ALRA, the UFW had the opportunity to be on the ballot if it submitted a petition with signatures from at least 20 percent of the company's workforce. The UFW refused to do this because, according to Rodriguez, "We have no interest in participating in a sham election that creates a mockery of protecting worker rights" (Rodebaugh 1998b). Jose Guadalupe Fernández defended the election, stating, "People here, people in the fields, we're tired of being 'educated' by the UFW. We want a chance to vote, and ... they should respect our decision" (Gaura 1998). That day, workers voted 523 to 410 in favor of the Comité.

The next day, at the height of the harvest season, hundreds of Coastal Berry workers walked off their jobs to protest the election. According to the company, almost two-thirds of the workforce was absent from the fields. The company accused the UFW of masterminding the walkout. The union countered the allegations, saying the walkouts were spontaneous and instigated by the workers themselves. Responding to the company claims, Rodriguez said, "That's a total lie. The workers came to us and said, 'That's it, we've had enough.' They've spoken very clearly that the election was a sham" (Associated Press 1998). Refusing to believe the UFW's version of events, Coastal Berry president David Smith said, "Quite frankly, the UFW is trying to punish us. They are trying to salvage an organizing campaign they sunk a lot of time and money into. But they've lost sight of the fact that only the workers can decide who will represent them. It's not up to the UFW" (Gaura 1998b).

The ALRB drew sharp criticism from labor leaders and lawmakers throughout the state for its decision to allow the election to proceed despite claims that the Comité was a sham and that it had engaged in violence and intimidation. Assemblyman Dick Floyd, chairman of the Assembly Labor and Employment Committee, denounced the board, stating, "What we are dealing with here is a lack of enforcement of the law of the state of California, nothing more, nothing less" (Lawrence 1998). ALRB general counsel Paul Richardson defended the board's decision to hold the election. He cited ALRB policy since 1982 to "vote now, litigate later." The policy had been implemented to ensure that court actions would not impede the wishes of workers to hold union elections. Addressing allegations of misconduct on the part of the Comité, Richardson went on to say, "We were fully prepared to investigate this case and ... make an appropriate assessment of where the truth was. But we cannot start issuing complaints ... when the rug is pulled out from under us two days before the election. It was difficult for us to assess the strength of the charges brought forth by the [UFW]." He added, "We have to give some credence (to the fact) that a majority of farm workers asked for an election" (ibid). In keeping with its pledge to consider the UFW's allegations, the board refused to certify the elections results until all complaints had been thoroughly investigated.

On July 31, the UFW presented the ALRB with an amendment to its motions to nullify the election. The union claimed that 162 workers from the company's Ventura County operation, nearly 15 percent of Coastal Berry's workforce, had not been notified of the election. By early August the ALRB had still not issued a ruling, stating that it needed more time to decide whether to certify the July 23 election results. According to Antonio Barbosa, the board's executive secretary, the UFW had raised some "novel legal issues" that required greater attention from the full board. In an interesting development, the owner of Coastal Berry, David Gladstone, filed his own objections to the election. The objections, similar to those of the UFW, stated that the Comité had created an atmosphere of fear and intimidation, that signatures on the election petition had been gathered illegally, and that workers in Ventura County had not been given the opportunity to vote.

By early September the ALRB had not yet issued a ruling. On September 14 the UFW protested outside the ALRB offices in Salinas, saying the board was dragging its feet in the investigation of objections to the election. One UFW supporter stated, "Something should be done for us now. We want this election thrown out so that we can organize without harassment" (Merrill 1998b). Several months passed before the board responded. On November 5 administrative law judge Thomas Sobel issued a preliminary decision voiding the Coastal Berry election. According to the ruling, the election was invalid because of the 162 workers in Ventura County who were not given the opportunity to vote. Reacting to the decision, Jose Guadalupe Fernández said, "The people spoke. For them [at the ALRB] to say we're going to throw out your election, I don't think that's right" (Henneman 1998).

Shortly after this ruling, on November 9, the UFW produced bank records to support its contention that industry groups had indeed supported anti-union efforts. According to bank statements, the Pro Workers Committee and several splinter organizations had received more than $56,000 in donations from growers and other agricultural interests. Among those implicated were the New West Fruit Corp, Del Llano farms, Saticoy Berry Farms in Oxnard, Watsonville Berry Cooler, Premier Growers Association, Clint Miller Farms, and the Western Growers Association. In early May 1999 the UFW announced that twenty growers and growers' groups who had funded anti-union groups had agreed to stop anti-UFW groups (UFW 1999). The UFW claimed that workers' committees were misrepresenting themselves by claiming to be independent when in fact they were financed by growers. To substantiate its claims, the UFW pointed to Jose Guadalupe Fernández, a prominent member of the now-defunct AWC and the current spokesperson for the Comité. The UFW indicated a connection between the Comité and grower support, although no evidence of the relationship was ever produced.[11] In a separate instance of litigation, Reiter Berry Farms, one of the largest suppliers of berries to Driscoll's, agreed to pay almost 500 berry pickers $283,000 for work without pay before and after shifts during the 1994–1997 seasons.

At the end of May 1999 there was a second vote for union recognition at Coastal Berry. The UFW had hoped to make gains in the company's Southern California operation, where it had recently been organizing extensively.[12] Centered in the north, the Comité only traveled to Ventura County a week or so before the election. The UFW's organizing in the south resulted in a strong showing; it received 309 votes as opposed to the Comité's 230. In the north, however, the UFW was overpowered by the Comité, which received 416 votes, compared to the UFW's 268. Sixty ballots remained disputed. The total vote was 646 to 577 in favor of the Comité, with 60 ballots unresolved and 79 ballots cast for "no union." Since no group received 682 votes, a majority, a runoff election was to be held several days later. For many supporters as well as critics of the UFW, this election was seen as a serious blow to the union's efforts to organize the industry.

A runoff election was held on June 3–4. The results of the election were 688 ballots in favor of the Comité and 598 ballots in favor of the UFW. Ninety-two ballots were disputed and thus had the potential to affect the outcome of the election. The harvesting season would nearly be over before a winner was announced. On August 17, near the end of the harvest season, the disputed ballots were resolved and the Comité was declared winner of the election. The final results were 725 ballots cast in favor of the Comité and 616 in favor of the UFW. The elections results were not considered conclusive, however. The UFW filed more than 200 objections to the election, charging a variety of election-day improprieties including voter coercion and intimidation. According to UFW spokesperson Marc Grossman, "This is just the beginning. Regardless of the outcome, the UFW will not be deterred from continuing to organize in the strawberry industry or other crops" (Alvarez 1999). Indeed, a final outcome would not be available until the following year.

On October 14, ALRB executive secretary Antonio Barboza ordered a December hearing to be held in Salinas to investigate objections to the Coastal Berry Company's election filed by the UFW. Barboza issued a report contending that nearly half of the UFW's 234 objections to the election warranted further review. However, the burden of proof for the charges of misconduct would lie with the UFW. Jim Gumberg, attorney for the Comité, accused the UFW of dragging out the process. "Of course the board grants them another month. They're trying to delay the inevitable" (Hanley 1999). Of the 234 objections to the election, the ALRB decided to send 100 to an administrative law judge. The UFW appealed the decisions concerning the remaining 134 objections.

Meanwhile, in the fields, workers were getting restless and were upset by the lengthy legal procedures that impeded the certification of the election results. According to Comité president Sergio Leal, "The people don't want another election. We already won three times. Why doesn't our vote count?" (Kleist 1999). Leal and his coworkers would have to wait until early 2000 to hear a definitive ruling.

Judge Thomas Sobel decided on March 7, 2000, to separate the company into two bargaining units. Workers in Ventura County would be represented by the UFW, and workers in Watsonville would have the Comité as their bargaining agent. The vote in the Ventura runoff election was 321 UFW to 277 Comité; in Watsonville the vote was 448 Comité to 295 UFW. The ruling temporarily ended major efforts by the UFW to organize the strawberry industry. Two years later, the UFW petitioned to organize Coastal Berry's Northern California operation. It beat the Comité in an ALRB-sponsored election. When the Comité did not contest the results, the UFW became the sole bargaining agent for workers at the Coastal Berry Company

The UFW unionization campaign in the Central Coast strawberry fields is the most recent contest in a long history of exchanges between labor and capital in California agriculture. In an interesting twist, however, the conflict that evolved did not pit growers against workers, as is usually the case. Rather, two groups both ostensibly fighting for workers' rights—organized labor and loosely organized workers—were now in contention. The UFW initiated the 1996 campaign as a large, highly organized, well-funded union with broad support from the state and the public sector. The Comité was the opposite—it even strained the definition of a formal organization. In the current situation, the UFW, usually presented as the underdog, took on the proverbial role of Goliath. Contrary to the biblical tale, however, this one ended in the victory of the larger, more powerful party.

To explore how the Comité was able to gain traction among workers at Coastal Berry, the next chapter takes a closer look at the interpersonal relations that existed among growers and farmworkers. Using the concept of social networks, I explain why some workers favored unionization while others did not. The chapter demonstrates how social networks can be obdurate social structures and why they can be overpowered by formal organizations in advanced industrial, liberal democracies.

---

[1] The political economy of agriculture emerged as a subfield of rural sociology in the 1970s. Rural sociology has historically focused on the social structure and social relations of agriculture. This new strain of rural sociology emphasizes relations of production in agrarian settings, the rise of commercial agriculture, socio-economic conditions of production, and environmental concerns in agriculture. The edited volumes by Buttel, Larson, and Gillespie (1990), and Friedland, Busch, Buttel, and Rudy (1991) exemplify research in this area. The edited volume by Chibnik (1987) presents similar studies from an anthropological perspective.

[2] My use of the term *state* draws from Dryzek et al. (2003), who define it as, "the set of individuals and organizations legally authorized to make binding decisions for a society within a particular territory" (p. 12). These binding decisions include public policy and legislation that constrain and enable the behaviors of individuals and collective actors.

[3] Using ALRA annual reports, Wells and Villarejo (2004) demonstrate that election petitions filed, elections held, and union-won elections were greatest in the act's first three years before declining precipitously. See figure 1, p. 301 (Wells and Villarejo 2004).

[4] Legal status has historically differentiated workers in the agriculture industry (Thomas 1985; Gonzales 1985).

[5] Punchers are workers who tally, either electronically or manually on a punch card, the number of boxes picked by a worker; hence, "puncher," or in Spanglish *ponchadora*. It is generally considered to be a relatively easy job and is highly coveted.

[6] My discussion of worker characteristics is based on my own observations, interviews with industry insiders, and Wells' (1996) interviews with farmworkers.

[7] The ALRB would later find the company had violated state labor laws, saying its action was retaliation against union organizing. The company agreed to a $113,000 settlement that was divided among some 300 employees, or between $400 and $450 per worker.

[8] A *notice to access* is filed with the ALRB when a union wishes to enter a grower's fields to talk to workers about unionization. A *notice to organize* indicates that a unionization drive is actually taking place. Notices to organize are usually filed after a union has secured a high level of support among workers. Unlike the National Labor Relations Act (NLRA), the ALRA stipulates that unions are entitled to access an employer's business premises (in this case the fields) by nonemployee labor representatives. The access clause is

often cited as the biggest point of contention between the grower community and the UFW.

[9] In the fall of 1997, less than half a year into their ownership of the company, David Gladstone bought out Landon Butler's 50 percent share of the Coastal Berry Company to become the sole owner.

[10] It is a common misperception among Mexican immigrants living in the United States that notarized documents are legally binding. It is perhaps because of this that workers at the company asked Smith to sign the document.

[11] My research did not reveal any financial or material support from growers to the Comité. It is unlikely that after being mired in expensive litigation for aiding previous anti-UFW groups that the grower community would have supported the Comité, even if they might have wanted to do so. Certainly the UFW and its supporters would not agree with my assertion that the Comité was neither backed by the industry nor a company union. UFW spokesperson Marc Grossman points to a 2000 6th District Court of Appeals decision, *United Farm Workers vs. Dutra Farms* (Case No. 133191), in which a link is made between various anti-UFW groups and several growers early in the strawberry campaign. The case specifically mentions the "Pro Workers [sic] Committee" (PWC) which in January of 1997 changed its name to the "Agricultural Workers of America" (AWA). The organization later became the "Agricultural Workers [sic] Committee," although it maintained the same address and officers as the previous group. The 6th District Court of Appeals decision states, "Hereafter, we refer to PWC, the AWC, and AWA as "the Committee." This should not be confused with the Comité, the Coastal Berry Farm Workers Committee. In fact, the Comité is never mentioned in this document. The organizations in the court decision were defunct by the time the Comité emerged. However, one individual was linked to both the earlier anti-UFW groups and the Comité. Jose Guadalupe Fernández was involved in the AWC and was a founding member of the Comité. Fernández would subsequently drop out of the Comité, but his involvement in both groups indicates to the UFW a clear and obvious link between the Comité and grower sponsorship. Other than the Fernández link, no evidence to date has been found that industry groups supported the *Comité* financially or materially as they did previous anti-UFW groups.

[12] The UFW did not organize in the southern part of the state from 1996 to 1998; instead it focused its attention on the northern Central Coast.

4

Immigrant Networks

In 1999, at the height of the UFW's organizing campaign at Coastal Berry, another instance of immigrant labor mobilization occurred south of the Pajaro Valley. In the southern Salinas Valley about 750 workers walked off their jobs at the Basic Vegetable Products Company in tiny King City (Cleeland 1999; Johnston 2004). After more than two months not one worker had returned to work at Basic. The company was forced to bus workers 55 miles across the Coastal Mountains from Coalinga. When asked about the strength of Basic's workers' solidarity, Teamsters Local 890 president Frank Gallegos responded, "They know the next hire could be their granddaughter. It's a very tight-knit group" (Cleeland 1999). Gallegos himself worked at Basic for thirteen years alongside his parents, a brother, an aunt, and several cousins. Industry insiders and researchers agree that family networks can be a powerful determinant of economic behavior among immigrants in the workforce. Family networks proved to be particularly durable at Basic. Over the course of the nearly two-year strike, only 7 percent of workers broke ranks and returned to work (Johnston 2004).[1]

Similar family networks influenced worker behavior at Coastal Berry during the UFW campaign. During the 2000 harvesting season I spoke with 20-year-old Mari Ortiz and her father, José, in their modest Watsonville apartment. José was a nominal supporter of the Comité, but only because he had worked in crews with Sergio Leal, one of the group's leaders. José's primary concern was steady employment, which he thought the Comité would ensure. Mari was neutral but told people she supported the Comité:

> Pensaban que yo era contraria pero o sea yo estaba neutral, no estaba ni pa'l comité ni pa' la unión. Pero ellos pensaban que yo estaba por el comité. Y yo para que no me estuvieran molestando les decía que si pero yo estaba neutral. O sea no estaba pa' ni uno ni otro. (They

thought I was against [the UFW] but I was neutral. I wasn't for the committee or the union. But they thought I was for the committee. And so they wouldn't bother me I said I was, but I was actually neutral.) [August 2000]

Mari worked at Coastal Berry with several of her cousins. When I asked her how she had obtained her job as a picker, she told me her father had helped her get the position. Given her relationship to her father and his connection with Sergio Leal, she would have found it difficult to support the UFW. Sergio's brother Enrique Leal was a supervisor at Coastal. Sergio Leal and Eddie Hernández, who had organizing experience in Mexico, were among the workers to start the Comité. Here, we can see how networks become embedded in the immigrant labor market and foster dynamics of worker loyalty to patrons through a multifaceted dynamic of dependence. At Coastal Berry the Leal family network fiercely opposed the UFW because the network and its supporters had the most to lose from a successful unionization campaign.

According to UC Berkeley geographer Harley Shaiken, "[Networks] are a powerful hidden dimension of immigration and, increasingly, labor relations. It's true all over the country, but particularly in California, where immigrant labor is vital to the economy and pivotal to the future of unions" (Cleeland 1999). Such networks facilitate employment for new and recent immigrants and serve as the primary context of socialization for immigrants. Consequently, networks can exert a great deal of pressure at the micro-sociological level of interpersonal interactions in the workplace. Depending on the situation, this pressure can be positive or negative for the well-being of individual immigrants within those networks.

Network theory is one component of my argument and is used to explain interpersonal interactions and labor market behavior among immigrant workers. This theoretical framework will also be employed to explain the development of "transnational communities," which serve as the broader socio-cultural context for immigrant labor mobilization. During periods of anti-immigrant sentiment such as that exhibited in California during the 1990s, family networks acquire added significance in the daily lives of workers. As we will see, networks can facilitate the transition of newly arrived immigrants into the American workforce and society. Networks can just as easily constrain the behavior of these immigrants once in the United States. This immigrant network dynamic is critical for understanding the initial rise of the Comité at Coastal Berry. However, networks only help to partially explain the Coastal

Berry case. Networks are very good at motivating people, but they not good at bringing about systemic change. To affect systemic social change, aggrieved groups must employ formal organizations, which are better able to influence the institutions that structure society. The UFW was eventually able to win a contract at Coastal Berry because it was a formal organization. Before this happened, however, the strength of interpersonal bonds among workers proved difficult for the UFW to overcome. Knowing how social networks function among immigrants helps us understand why this was the case.

Social Network Theory

Basic, Coastal Berry, and many other workplaces that employ immigrant labor provide salient examples of social networks and their impacts on individual behavior in the labor market. A *social network* comprises interpersonal ties that connect individuals or organizations (Granovetter 1973).[2] A tie connects Mari to her father José. Mari, José, and Sergio Leal, the Comité leader, form a simple network. Social interactions among network members transmit various types of information. Theorists describe the information available within networks as social capital that functions as an asset or resource (Lin 1999). A person in a network accesses such information via his or her location in the network.[3] The information can then be used to the person's advantage in various ways. Family networks have historically facilitated access to elite universities in the United States and Great Britain, though they do so to a lesser extent now (Soares 1999). More recently, scholars have examined the ways in which social capital found in personal networks affects job opportunities (Burt 1997; Portes and Sensenbrenner 1993; Waldinger and Lichter 2003). Mari and many others at Coastal Berry, Basic, and other companies obtained employment when they learned of an opening through a close friend or family member.

Nan Lin (1999) theorizes about how individuals can use social capital for personal gain or status enhancement within hierarchical social networks constituted by weak ties. Burt expands on this version of social capital with a theory of structural holes (1997). A *structural hole* is a gap presenting an opportunity for an individual to "broker the flow of information between people and control the form of projects that bring people together from opposite sides of the hole" (1997: 455). This social entrepreneur functions as an intermediary between networks or organizations. One example might be a college president. Another would be a senior-level supervisor at a crop harvesting company. An individual who serves as a bridge between networks or organizations accrues valuable information and social power as a result of his or her strategic social location. These benefits and control help to explain why people in such positions seek to maintain them. Social entrepreneurs who served as network brokers were prominent actors in the Coastal Berry campaign. Sergio's brother Enrique is a prime example because it was thought that he controlled worker access and well-being at the company. His position was so powerful that when critics accused the Comité of being a company union, they were really attacking his power and that of other supervisors.

The existence of vertical social contacts implies a hierarchy of social power. Weber defines *social power* as the ability of an individual or group to impose its will on others, even in the face of resistance (in Gerth and Mills 1946). Sergio had social power over José, Mari, and others because of his access to his brother Enrique, who held more social power than Sergio because of his structural position within the company. Social capital and social power within networks is a particularly significant feature of life for immigrant groups. Most people belong to multiple overlapping networks of family, friends, and work associates. Recent immigrants may not belong to such extensive networks. For them, networks may be more tightly bound to family and kin-like relations.

Because of their marginalized social position and informal political status, immigrant workers must rely heavily on family networks for social capital. A sense of group solidarity develops and then increases during periods of hostility toward recognizable immigrant groups. This phenomenon has been identified by previous immigration scholars. "[The] more distinct a group is in terms of phenotypical or cultural characteristics from the rest of the population," Alejandro Portes and Julia Sensenbrenner argue, "the greater the level of prejudice associated with these traits, and the lower the probability of exit from this situation, then the stronger the sentiments of in-group solidarity among its members and the higher the appropriable social capital based on this solidarity" (1993: 1329). This was the case in California during the 1990s when strong anti-Latino immigrant sentiment culminated politically in 1994 with Proposition 187, which sought to severely limit social services including health care and education to undocumented persons.

Social Networks and Economic Behavior

For recent immigrants, family networks are quite likely to influence work, friends, and other spheres of social life. When employment is a primary objective, as it usually is for immigrants, access to someone like Enrique acquires special significance. People such as Enrique mediate labor-market exchanges between workers and employers. His relationships with other workers are shaped by his structural position within the company, and those relationships influence the behavior of other workers. This view contradicts theories that present market exchanges as on-the-spot transactions between parties motivated primarily by self-interest. It does not, however, support the view that solidarity in the workplace will necessarily arise from collective interests based on economically similar positions.

Participation in strawberry production is economic behavior. Farmers grow berries to sell at commercial produce markets. Farmworkers working in the berry fields participate in the labor market. Economic behavior in markets is often discussed in terms of self-interest or class interests. Adam Smith's classic liberal view would emphasize the self-interested behavior of individuals participating in temporary market exchanges. In *The Wealth of Nations* he writes, "What are the common wages of labor depends every where upon the contrast usually made between those two parties, whose interests are by no means the same. The workmen desire to get as much, the masters to give as little as possible" (Heilbroner: 83–84). At the other end of the theoretical spectrum, Karl Marx considered work to be a profoundly social activity and sought to explain the inevitable development of collective action based on economic group interest. He writes, "The collisions between individual workmen and individual bourgeois take more and more the character of collisions between two classes" (Tucker 1978: 17–18). According to many theorists, common awareness of capitalist exploitation leads to solidarity among individuals similarly positioned in the labor market.[4]

Although both perspectives are not necessarily wrong, they are also not quite right either. Individual economic behavior takes shape within the context of established social relations. From this perspective we see that notions of individual "self-interest" acquire meaning within social networks. As David Snow writes, "material conditions like economic deprivation or unemployment are themselves subject to differential interpretation and therefore do not automatically constitute or generate mobilizing grievances" (2007: 382–383). So while market-based labor mobilization does occur, it is not always driven automatically or principally by material self-interest. Other values or ideals take precedence according to one's structural position within a network. For individuals with strong network ties, these conventions will influence action by providing cognitive schemas to interpret behavior and interests.[5] What Snow (2007) refers to as "signifying work" or meaning construction occurs within networks and influences the subjective interpretation of objective conditions. Portes and Sensenbrenner refer to such schema as "those expectations for action within a collectivity that affect the economic goals and goal seeking behavior of its members, even if these expectations are not oriented toward the economic sphere" (1993: 1323). In a labor market, one would expect to see market-associated values such as individualism and earnings maximization as individuals compete to sell berries and buy and sell labor. Rather, individuals draw on network ties, acting in ways that defy collective economic behavior or material self-interest.

Labor market transactions represent established patterns of social interaction. Economic behavior within these markets is social behavior that must be understood with reference to the exercise of social power and the influence of cultural conventions that function within networks. Over time, interactions within and between networks give rise to patterns of interaction and the development of cultural forms that serve as guidelines for behavior. Such patterns arise not only within networks but also between networks. In agricultural labor markets, for instance, continuous interactions between growers and farmworkers give rise to certain norms and patterns of interaction between these groups; patterns of interaction evolve *within* farmer and farmworker groups as well. These interactional dynamics have operated historically among the various ethnic groups involved in the industry.

When Japanese farmers began to move out of sharecropping and into independent farming after World War II, they called upon family members for supervisory and harvest positions (Wells 1996). More recently, poorly capitalized Mexican farmers have done the same with their kin. In these instances family bonds within the workplace can undermine the possibility of collective behavior based on similar economic positions. Today, most operators do not rely on their kin for labor, yet networks continue to influence labor market exchanges.

Strawberry operations in the Pajaro Valley can be divided into three general categories based on size and profitability. The first, least profitable category includes independent farmers, usually former immigrant workers operating on farms smaller than 40 acres. These farmers are least likely to belong to a growing-and-shipping cooperative. The next category includes farms employing eighty to two hundred workers at the peak of the season, depending on the acreage of the operation (personal communication David Riggs, 20 October 2000). The bulk of strawberry operations in California fall into this category. Operations in this range can foster bonds of familiarity and trust between farmworkers and farmers over multiple harvest seasons. A manager at one large operation told me proudly, "We have less annual turnover than Safeway" (October 2000). The final category includes the largest operations—those over 300 acres in size. The largest operations are also the best capitalized. Like medium-sized operators, farmers in this category are likely to be members of a grower-shipper facility. Coastal Berry was an anomaly in two notable respects: it had the largest workforce, 1,200 workers; and it vertically integrated its operations by running its own cooler and shipper operation. It was a behemoth in an industry that tended to operate on a much smaller scale.

Network relationships function differently depending on the size and management structure of an operation. Small- and medium-sized operations are likely to foster strong interpersonal relationships between farmers and farmworkers. An operation as large as Coastal Berry requires a complex management structure. Here the position of social entrepreneur is usually formalized through his or her particular position within the company hierarchy. When this happens, as it does at many berry operations, preexisting kinship ties are further cemented.

Before focusing the campaign on Coastal Berry, the UFW targeted farmers who were members of the large grower-shipper companies in the region. These farmers produced for the high-end market and paid their employees accordingly. Workers at these operations enjoyed relatively good wages, and most had benefits. Workers at the smallest operations, where profit margins were slim, suffered the most from deplorable working conditions. These undercapitalized farmers were usually Mexican and often relied on family members to fill harvest positions. It was these growers whom Miriam Wells had in mind when she wrote, "All producers benefit from the downward pressure on wages and working conditions that such a labor supply exerts, but many small, low-resource producers require it as a condition of survival" (1996: 65). These farmers were the ones most likely to try to increase their already slim profit margins by cutting the cost of labor through various means. They were least likely to provide benefits, for instance. They also relied most heavily on family connections for labor. Thus, the workers most in need of labor union protection were also the most likely to resist unionization because of preexisting bonds of kinship.

Close working relationships among farmers and farmworkers at many operations throughout the Pajaro Valley complicated the UFW organizing campaign. A successful UFW campaign would need to alter these network ties. When I asked Elida Vasquez, a former farmworker and current farmer, about the relationships between her and workers at her farm, she responded, "You get to know the families and their problems. You're with them when their kids go to college, when they graduate, when they lose family members, when they get married. I have close relations with my workers" (October 2000).

I found Vasquez's experiences to be fairly typical for mid-size farm operators in the area. Had these bonds been weak, as they might have been at operations with high turnover, or lacking extensive kinship ties, the union could have found a following in the workforce. Instead, the UFW had difficulty organizing on most farms in the Pajaro Valley. According to a long-time resident and local Latino politician,

> Around here, you have farmers who have been very good to their workers. You have farmers who have helped them buy homes. You have farmers who have supplied them with health insurance and other benefits.... I think what's happened is when people have worked for companies for years and those companies have taken care of you for years, it's really hard to build a wedge against those companies that treat their workers good. (May 2000)

The only farmer in the Central Coast strawberry industry whose operation was unionized was Jim Cochran, who grew a variety of organic crops including berries in the hills north of Santa Cruz, well outside the Pajaro Valley. Even he conceded, "When the UFW first came out, many guys were scared, and rightfully so I think" (October 2000). For Cochran, however, unionization was as much an ethical issue as it was a pragmatic business decision. He considered farmworkers skilled employees and thought that they should have health care. "There is nothing wrong with being a farmworker. It's a dignified occupation. So why not help create that feeling of professionalism?" (October 2000). For Cochran, this meant providing employees with health care. The small size of his operation made doing so economically difficult, however. Cochran thought of himself as a manager of a business operation, and unionization could provide workers on his farm with health care. He presented the idea to workers, and they readily agreed to unionization.

Cochran was geographically removed from the Pajaro Valley and had only weak ties to the farmer networks there. He knew a few farmers in the Watsonville area, but because he farmed north of Santa Cruz and because he did not belong to a cooler-shipper, his contact with Pajaro Valley farmers was limited.

About 80 percent of berries are sold through companies that prepare and ship fruit (Wells 1996). Early in the development of the modern berry-growing industry, individuals in family networks created cooperative business organizations to handle the capital-intensive tasks of preparing and selling berries to global markets. Once picked, berries must be rapidly cooled to 33 degrees and properly stored to extend shelf life. This process requires large cooling facilities and transportation systems. Cooperatives cool, store, and market strawberries for their members.

The three largest cooperatives—Driscoll Strawberry Associates, Naturipe Berry Growers, and Watsonville Berry Cooperative—were started by individuals in ethnically organized grower networks. Naturipe, one of the earliest marketing cooperatives, was founded by white and Japanese growers in 1917. The Watsonville Berry Cooperative was started by a kin-based network of Japanese farmers in the 1950s. Driscoll Berry Associates was founded by white farmers who had left Naturipe to start their own cooler-shipper. Kinship ties within these cooler-shippers traversed generations. Two of the five founders of Driscoll's—Edward and Donald Driscoll—were brothers. Miles Reiter, who was Driscoll's president during the UFW campaign, is the son of Joe Reiter, another of the cooperative's founders.

Membership in ethnically based family networks influences individual farmers' profitability. In a study released immediately prior to the UFW organizing campaign, Wells (1996) examined the relationship between co-op membership, ethnicity, and profit margins. She found that Mexican growers are least likely to belong to a grower-shipper or cooperative organization and have the least access to capital.[6] White farmers had the greatest access to capital and were most likely to belong to grower-shippers or cooperatives. Furthermore, white farmers held the best lands (and paid the highest rents for them) and offered the highest wages. They also had the highest investment and return per acre of all farmers.[7] Wells's study confirms that network ties have real material outcomes. Farmers make use of the social capital available to them through their networks to access valuable information on farming practices, credit sources, and favorable terms of membership to cooperatives or cooler shippers. Farmers without such extensive vertical social ties, usually Mexican, can fall into exploitive relationships with independent shippers, who also act as lending agents to poorly capitalized farmers.

Between 1970 and 1987, the demand for strawberries increased by over 50 percent (Wells 1996). During this period the number of local shippers more than doubled (ibid). Initially, local shippers had difficulty finding fruit because most well-established high-volume growers belonged to cooperatives or grower-shipper associations and sold their crops to these groups. In response to the increased demand, local shippers turned to the experienced farmworkers, for it suddenly became profitable to finance new growers to meet the growing demand for strawberries. With their intimate understanding of strawberry cultivation, farmworkers were the obvious candidates for these new arrangements. These workers were eager to become their own bosses, so many entered into contracts with shippers.

Because it is possible to farm successfully on plots smaller than 20 acres, kinship relations can be used to reduce the cost of labor (only 1.5 to 2 pickers are needed per acre during peak season). Furthermore, greater yields and higher quality can be achieved through greater care and attention to the crop. Since the early 1900s, these factors have created openings for various ethnic minority and immigrant groups to start their own operations in the industry. When strawberry production increased in the 1970s and 1980s due to expanding markets, Mexican Americans took advantage of the relatively low entry barriers and joined whites and Japanese as growers.

Entry-level growers and those who were undercapitalized often entered inequitable relationships with commercial shippers.[8] Because these farmers lacked the financial resources or legitimacy to secure credit, they turned to shippers to finance their operations. A shipper would supply money to rent land, equipment, seed, and fertilizer. In exchange, the grower agreed to sell the berries to the shipper at a preset price. Profits from sales were split according to a predetermined formula. Acting as financiers, shippers provided high-interest loans at the beginning of each season to cover production costs. Growers were responsible for repayment even if the harvest was not profitable. It was thus easy for such growers to fall into a cycle of debt to shippers. As independent operators, these farmers were also responsible for the overall management of berry production. Therefore, shippers did not have to address issues of immigration or labor. According to Wells (1996), most, if not all, growers involved in these types of relationships were former Mexican origin strawberry workers. These arrangements continue to be a major force shaping the social relationships of the strawberry industry.

Of course, not all Mexican origin farmers are poorly capitalized and exploited. Mexican immigrant Jesus Cornejo grew up picking strawberries alongside his parents. After attending Cal Poly San Luis Obispo, he returned to the Pajaro Valley, where he began leasing land to grow his own berries. At the time I interviewed him he was a member of a cooler-shipper, and he enjoyed moderate success. But farmers like Jesus Cornejo and Elida Vasquez were more the exception than the norm. It was quite common for workers to begin leasing a few acres with the hope of becoming individual proprietors only to fail and go into debt. Even though the odds were against them, many workers saw this as a path toward prosperity and independence from day labor. In the Pajaro Valley, however, it was difficult for a former farmworker to thrive as a farmer.

Social Networks and the Organization of Production

As in most workforces that rely heavily on undocumented immigrant labor, family networks are extremely valuable in the strawberry industry. Nearly every worker I interviewed obtained employment through a friend or relative.[9] Many workers on individual farms are members of extended family networks. Workers not related to other workers tend to be single males. Kinship and friendship networks play an important role in the industry workforce. Farmers rely heavily on these networks for recruitment during the harvest. Conversely, family groups work to establish and maintain relationships with certain farmers over several seasons. These relationships can be used to secure employment for new friends or family members. Older, more established workers who are part of a core workforce introduce and vouch for new recruits. This approach provides a greater sense of legitimacy for prospective employees than would simply having them walk to the edge of a field asking for work. Because experienced workers value their relationships with their bosses, they are likely to ensure the training and ultimate success of workers they recommend.

Family networks ease the transition for recently arrived immigrants. In fact, many workers belong to pre-established kin and quasi-kin networks even before they arrive at the Central Coast.[10] Kin already established in the US may provide a loan to help pay for the trip, including the smuggler's fee. Kin also help recent immigrants become established in the local area by providing housing and job-search assistance, which often means securing a position for the recent immigrant at the farm where the family is already employed. In exchange for this readily available support network, the newly arrived immigrant is expected to extend a certain degree of respect and loyalty to the leader of the group.

Kinship groups generally include one or two de facto leaders. These leaders are usually those who have been in the United States for the longest time and are considered the head (or *cacique*) of the group. While they may be pickers, they tend to be in managerial positions in local farms or are at least employed on a year-round basis. They are usually better off economically than others in their group and may even own a small home. This relative degree of affluence allows them to provide for the extended kin group financially, usually through small loans. Lending to fellow workers further solidifies the leadership position of these individuals within the extended network. Due to the constant flow of people between Mexico and the United States, *caciques* wield influence over their group in the Central Coast as well as in the community of origin. Over time, *caciques* and their kin have come to play a critical role in the Central Coast strawberry industry. Although the term was not employed by the workers themselves, the concept of the *cacique* helps explain the patron-client dynamic within social networks and the way in which clientelistic relations impact the decision-making processes of individual workers.

Caciques and Kin

Among Mexican immigrants these arrangements are the basis for a system of patronage. When a recent arrival has been successfully transitioned into the host community, he or she is then indebted to the sponsor. This indebtedness is further cemented if the sponsor is in some way responsible for the employment of the immigrant. Many sponsors are entrepreneurial, running small businesses in which recent arrivals are likely to be employed. When they are not business proprietors, many sponsors nevertheless have access to jobs because they hold managerial positions. In the agriculture industry a managerial position is particularly useful to a patron because of the high demand for labor. Even if the sponsor is not able to hire the new arrival immediately, he or she may facilitate employment through access to a greater network of potential employers. Either way, new immigrants are in debt, symbolically if not financially, to their sponsors. If a job is not procured directly through the patron, the newly arrived immigrant still has certain obligations to the patron. The initial sponsorship often requires some degree of investment, financial or otherwise, on the part of the sponsor. Furthermore, the newly arrived immigrant remains dependent on the sponsor for a variety of day-to-day needs in the new country. These arrangements create bonds of reciprocity that are strengthened as the new arrival's stay in the country continues.

Douglas Massey and colleagues note that "typically someone from the sending community achieves a position of responsibility that enables him or her to channel employment, housing, and other resources to fellow townspeople" (1994: 1501). The role of these patrons in the migrant circuit is analogous to the role of the Latin American *cacique*. The term *cacique* is usually applied in reference to people in Latin

America, specifically Mexico.[11] Historically, *caciques* were able to exert control over others through their positions as intermediaries between villagers and national sources of economic and political power. The relationship between a *cacique* and his followers is characterized by unequal exchange (Pit-Rivers 1954; Wolf 1966).[12] The *cacique* ensures that his followers have the vital resources necessary for survival, and they in turn offer their political allegiance and loyalty.

Writing about the ties of patronage that buttress such a system, Eric Wolf notes, "Such ties would prove especially functional in situations where the formal institutional structure of society is weak and unable to deliver a sufficiently steady supply of goods and services, especially to the terminal levels of the social order" (1966: 17). These relationships operate because the limited points of access to political and economic resources are controlled by the *cacique*. Because of this, the *cacique* has a vested interest in the status quo. Any change in the political system threatens the monopoly the *cacique* has over access to resources and therefore power. Thus, any disruption of the status quo in which *caciques* maintain social control will be met with resistance by people threatened with a loss of power, including individuals who benefit personally from their close social ties to the *cacique*. This phenomenon can be observed at Coastal Berry and at other employers with large immigrant workforces.

According to my research, some workers in the agriculture industry have adopted roles much like that of *caciques*—power brokers and intermediaries between kin and resources. These people enjoy the greater access to resources necessary for the successful transition of workers from immigrants to wage earners. Most notable of their capacities is access to employment. As noted by Massey and his colleagues, "Family and friendship connections build up among migrants with time, therefore providing aspirants with a kind of 'social capital' they can draw upon to begin a migrant career" (1987: 150). In their study of how jobs were obtained by immigrants from four Mexican communities, referral by a friend or relative ranged from 29.4 percent to 45.6 percent of all modes of employment access (1987: 151). Successful entry into the US labor market is therefore highly dependent on the interpersonal ties migrants have with established friends and relatives.

Social network connections are especially important in the agriculture industry, where personal contacts are critical for job placement (Massey et al. 1994). People in managerial positions become gatekeepers to employment as well as promotion. Managers and foremen also act as arbiters between growers and laborers at worksites. These *cacique*-like individuals wield an enormous amount of power over their subordinates at work. Control over workers often extends beyond the workplace, though. Having few resources and living in a foreign land, often vulnerable because of their immigration status, recent arrivals are highly dependent on managers for various necessities of life. Workers may make commuter arrangements through their managers, for instance. Managers are often partially or fully responsible for the newcomer's lodging and commonly welcome the latter into their own homes or rent a place for them elsewhere. When an immigrant has entered the country illegally, as is overwhelmingly the case in the agriculture industry, such arrangements are critical to the recent arrival's successful transition to the labor force.

In the agriculture industry, the workers most likely to attain positions of power and become *caciques* are those who have established themselves in the receiving community. Over time, these individuals have been able to set up contacts with potential employers. Through their extended experience living in the United States, the *caciques* also have access to information important to recent immigrants: information about health care, social services, and legal issues. Sharing this information with recent arrivals creates bonds of obligation between the two parties and strengthens the immigrant network.

Not every immigrant will establish a relationship with a *cacique*-like figure. Furthermore, while these *caciques* tend to be kin relations, they are not necessarily so. New arrivals are, however, likely to be highly dependent on their kin for necessary resources. Recent immigrants take advantage of their relationships with more established members of their kin groups to facilitate a successful transition to the United States. Initially, the day-to-day lives of immigrants are highly determined by the limits of their kinship sphere. As immigrants settle into life in a host society, they begin to expand their network of contacts beyond the initial sphere of kinship. This may take place at work with the development of non-kin ties with other immigrants, or *paisanos* (countrymen). As newly arrived immigrants extend their social networks and become settled in a receiving community, they begin to loosen the bonds that initially tied them to their *cacique*. They are no longer as dependent on their patrons for their well-being and are thus not as indebted to them.

The more time an immigrant spends in the receiving society, the more his or her personal network extends beyond the kin group. This social network extension does not imply loss of contact with kin. Kin group members continue to play an important role in the life of an immigrant. Kinship bonds will be renewed and strengthened at life-course events such as weddings, baptisms, *quinceañeras*, and other important festivals. The nature of these bonds, however, shifts away from the unequal terms of exchange that characterized the initial patron-client relations. As the individual's network ties expand, he or she becomes less dependent on each individual person in the network. While continuing to view the initial patron as an important relation, an immigrant will broaden his or her resource base beyond that single individual or the kin group.

Immigrant network ties are not exclusively positive and beneficial. Many scholars and observers have written about the negative aspects of social networks, particularly in labor market situations. According to Portes and Sensenbrenner, "The same social mechanisms that give rise to appropriable resources for individual use can also constrain action or even derail it from its original goals" (1993: 1338). Such constraints on individual decisions can have especially pernicious effects on unionization campaigns. UFW spokesperson Marc Grossman has said, "It's an exploitive relationship. The power the foremen and supervisors have is a function of favoritism, bringing on their relatives and people from their hometowns. They have a stake in the union not being there because that's something we do away with immediately" (Cleeson 1999). In her study of undocumented Mexican and Central American immigrants in the Los Angeles janitorial industry, Cynthia Cranford (2005) found that social networks facilitated worker exploitation and the downgrading of work. She concludes that it is important to consider the industrial context of work to determine the extent to which social capital within networks will help or hinder workers in the workplace. This is especially relevant to the Coastal Berry case, where social networks embedded within the organizational structure of the company heavily impacted individual workers' views regarding unionization.

Individual workers at Coastal Berry similarly experienced the negative aspects of social networks. Doña Tere Delgadillo was the oldest farmworker I interviewed. She came to the United States in 1972 and had been working in the fields ever since. Her story exemplifies the power of personal relations in the California strawberry industry. Since 1983 she had worked as a strawberry picker at the company that would eventually become Coastal Berry, yet in that time she never rose above the rank of picker to occupy the more coveted position of ticket puncher. When I asked her why she had never been promoted, she responded,

> Hay mucha discriminación en la compañía, porque si tú tienes alguien que te apoye, tu andas que ponchadora. Que tengas tu relacionado a un mayordomo, te van subiendo tu señoría.... Allí no te dan ninguna oportunidad de nada. Solamente que tu tengas alguien que sea tu

escalera para poder subir al nivel que quieres. (There is a lot of discrimination in the company because if you have someone who supports you, you will be a puncher. If you are related to a foreman, that relation increases your seniority. They don't give you any opportunity to do anything there. Only if you have someone who will be your ladder can you reach the level you want.) [August 2000]

Doña Tere had experienced the negative power of social networks in the workplace firsthand. Early on, she became an ardent supporter of the UFW.

Another worker who experienced the negative impacts of patron-client relations within social networks was Juan Corona. Originally from Mexico City, Juan did not have family members working at Coastal Berry, but it was quite evident to him that kin and kin relations worked against him at the company. He stated,

> Nunca le dan a uno la oportunidad de progresar. Prefieren al amigo que acaba de llegar, o al primo, o al hermano. Los mayordomos y todos esos tienen como quien dice una dinastía, de que salgo yo pero dejo a mi primo. (They never give you the opportunity to progress. They prefer the friend who just arrived [from Mexico] or the cousin, or the brother. The foremen and the rest of them have what you might call a dynasty, in that they might vacate a post, but they'll leave their cousin [working there]). [October 2000]

Like Doña Tere, Juan Corona eventually became a supporter of the UFW. As a worker not aligned with a dominant family network at the company, he was less bound by patron-client relations. He was, however, also less likely to be promoted or to receive preferential treatment. For workers like Corona, the UFW offered greater opportunities for occupational mobility.

Whether positive or negative, social networks are an integral part of the lives of immigrant workers in the United States. According to Massey and his colleagues, Mexico-US migration patterns have become institutionalized to the point that the process is an integral element of social and economic life in both countries. They write, "Kinship forms one of the most important bases of migrant social organization, and family connections are the most secure bonds within the networks" (1987: 140). Over time, networks may become embedded within certain industries and particular companies as a result of network referrals for job openings and the placement of co-ethnics in supervisory positions. These networks can facilitate labor needs for employers, but as Cranford (2005) and Roger Waldinger and Michael Lichter (2003) have demonstrated, they can also operate to the detriment of both individual workers and companies. Both positive and negative aspects of social networks in the workplace were evident at Coastal Berry.

For many years strong family networks functioned to satisfy the labor requirements at Coastal Berry. By brokering access to coveted jobs, *caciques* and their immediate supporters also benefited from this arrangement because it ensured the loyalty and deference of workers who had obtained positions through network ties. Thus, before the unionization campaign there was a confluence of interests between established family networks and the company's bottom line. This arrangement changed when a unionization campaign threatened the power of those networks. When the UFW began campaigning at Coastal Berry, influential persons within those networks worked to undermine the company's support of the UFW, which in turn significantly disrupted production and therefore profitability at the company.

The Leal family network in particular featured prominently in anti-UFW resistance. But the original Comité comprised workers from different networks as well as workers only loosely affiliated with the Leal or Lobato families. According to the story told to Marc Lifsher, a *Wall Street Journal* reporter, the Comité was started at the end of a working day by a tired bunch of strawberry pickers. At the edge of a nameless strawberry field, Eddie Hernández drew a line in the soil. He urged workers in favor of the UFW to step across the line. He then asked workers who were tired of the UFW and who were willing to stand against the union to stay on his side of the line. About ten people moved across the line, and 350 remained on his side. According to Lifscher's report, that was the birth of the Comité. Over the next two picking seasons, a core group of fifteen organizers met frequently after work. As the group grew, it began to meet in a local park in Watsonville. Two seasons later, the recently formed workers' committee asked the California Agricultural Labor Relations Board for an election at the company. Although the actual story may not be as dramatic as that recounted to Lifsher, what the Comité did in the summer of 1999 was no different from what countless groups of immigrant workers have done in American labor markets: they organized to protect what they perceived to be their interests.

Family networks are complex social structures. Among recent immigrant working in the California agriculture industry, family networks are a lifeline. It is often through family networks that immigrants arrive in the United States, find a job, and get settled into their new society. However, the same network bonds that ease the transition to a new country can also constrain a person's actions. Bonds of deference and loyalty are not easily broken. Their durability has significant implications in the workplace where individual decision making is heavily influenced by network values and interests. At Coastal Berry, kin and kin-like ties discouraged many people from supporting the UFW. These network ties facilitated the emergence of the Comité. Nevertheless, as the next chapter demonstrates, however durable social networks may be, they are limited compared to the power of formal organizations.

---

[1] Johnston (2004) provides an account of the successful strike at Basic that draws on social movement theory, organizational analysis, and the sociology of power.

[2] The primary unit of analysis in this chapter is the individual.

[3] It is important to distinguish between social capital and human capital. *Human capital* can be described as the skills, abilities, and experiences that an individual can offer in exchange for wages in a labor market situation. *Social capital* refers to salient information generated and circulated within networks to which individuals have access. It may be said that social capital mediates the return on human capital.

[4] Historically, Marxian literature has divided these two groups into categories known as labor and capital. *Capital* refers to those who own the means of production, including things like property, machinery, and technology. People who do not own the means of production sell their *labor* on the labor market. I depart from this economistic conceptualization of class and borrow Wilson's Weberian definition of class as a group that has more or less similar services, goods, or skills to offer for income in a given economic order. Members of a class will receive similar financial remuneration for these services, goods, or skills, and class position will determine one's life chances and possibilities for personal life experiences (1980).

[5] According to Granovetter, four factors determine the strength of an interpersonal tie: time, emotional intensity, intimacy, and reciprocity (1973).

[6] While none of the white or Japanese farmers borrowed from shippers, over half of the Mexican growers did (Wells 1996: 121).

[7] According to a 1993 survey by UC Davis's Rural Migration Program, white farmers averaged $25,000 in gross revenue per acre, Japanese averaged $20,000, and Mexicans averaged $12,000.

[8] For a more detailed discussion of sharecropping in the California strawberry industry see Wells (1984; 1996, chapters 7 and 8); and Schlosser (1995).

[9] This point is bolstered by Wells's findings in the mid-1980s that 93 percent of strawberry workers' kin or friends helped in finding work.

[10] It is sometimes the case that members of family groupings are not related by kinship ties. They may be neighbors or close friends in their home villages and maintain relationships that are kinship-like in nature.

[11] Anthropologists and political scientists use the term *cacique* to refer to indigenous leaders who can be military chiefs, landowners who control a specified region, or any other local power broker (Wolf and Hansen 1967; Scott 1977; Schwerin 1973). After the Mexican Revolution ended in 1917, indigenous

bosses were able to consolidate their power over local areas through their connections to the national political system (Friedrich 1968, 1977). Their connections to the national political apparatus allowed them to obtain resources for their supporters. The resultant patron-client relations have historically been prevalent in regions where the state apparatus was weak and access to resources limited. Rural areas in Mexico were most likely to engender this type of exchange, but the phenomenon has also been observed in poor urban areas (Cornelius 1977; Hansen 1971). Thus, as Villarreal writes, "Consolidation of a competitive electoral system with effective alternation of parties in office will weaken the power of a *cacique* because he will no longer be able to control the distribution of state resources and political influence on which his power depends" (2002: 481). In his study on the relationship between electoral competition and homicide in Mexico, Villarreal found that when electoral competition increased in areas where patron-client structures were strongest, homicide rates increased.

[12] It is interesting to note that in the literature, *caciques* are always male. This is not to say that a similar position could not be held by a woman.

5

Institutional Inclusion and the Organization of Dissent

The strength of interpersonal social networks explains the initial popularity of the Comité, but networks alone do not explain the outcome of labor organizing at Coastal Berry. Networks are only part of the reason that the UFW eventually was able to win a labor contract at Coastal Berry and the Comité ultimately failed. More important to the outcome of labor organizing at Coastal Berry is that the UFW was a formal organization, and the Comité was not. Effective organizations are the vehicles by which marginalized groups affect social change. Organizations provide groups of people with similar interests opportunities for sustained interactions with the civic and political institutions that shape societies and individual lives. The Comité's failure to transition from a group of similarly minded workers to a formal labor union explains its inability to continue its successes in Coastal Berry's strawberry fields. In contrast, the UFW formalized itself as an organization in the late 1960s and early 1970s, early in its history. Its initial victories and the institutionalization of its gains can be attributed to this formalization, which allowed it to effectively compete against other established organizations beginning in the 1960s.

A study of the internal structures of the Comité, the UFW, and the Coastal Berry Company illustrates the importance of *organizational capacity*—an organization's ability to successfully interact with other organizations that constitute the civic and political institutions of a society. Organizational capacity is contingent on the level of formalization within an organization. The Comité remained loosely structured throughout the strawberry campaign and was thus unable to develop its organizational capacity. Organizational capacity in itself does not assure an organization's success, however. The UFW and Coastal Berry were highly organized and still exhibited certain dysfunctional aspects, as we will see. Lack of organizational capacity, however, almost certainly guarantees failure in the long term.

The Comité struggled to transform itself into a professional labor union in the months following the May 2000 judicial decision to split Coastal Berry into two bargaining units for the purposes of union representation. A formal organizational structure was necessary for the union to implement a variety of standardized processes to bolster or replace previous company policies, which had been lax, neglected, or nonexistent. The new procedures and capacities included a formal grievance policy and procedure, a system of promotion and demotion, and importantly, a hiring hall. As lawyer Jim Lorenz put it, "We have to formalize the informal." He conceded that it was not an easy task. "We've never done this before," he said (December 2000). Comité members found it difficult to attend regularly scheduled board meetings, read the new contract, and introduce new policies to Coastal Berry's workers. The Comité and its directors also had to learn how to conduct themselves as a professional union in their interactions with other organizations including the company, the Agricultural Labor Relations Board, the press, and the general public.

The Comité's development as a formal organization in its dealings with Coastal Berry and other bureaucratized groups was a work in progress. Earnie Farley, president of the company, mentioned that early meetings with the group were chaotic and included large numbers of people. "I can't negotiate with 30 guys," he said (October 2000). But Farley also mentioned that Lorenz and employees from the company's payroll office were helping the group get organized. Enrique Leal acknowledged that "everything that we are doing now is by the book, by the law. We didn't want to do it this way but we had to" (December 2000). Learning about formal procedures that govern the internal and external work of organizations was a new activity for the group. The Comité had become part of a community of organizations and found itself uncomfortable and struggling in its new role.

Formal organizations are the building blocks of institutional life, which comprises interactions among organizations. For analytical purposes it is useful to distinguish between that which occurs *within* organizations and exchanges *among* organizations. Individual organizations are the basic unit of analysis here and serve as this chapter's foci of discussion. Before organizations can successfully participate institutionally—that is, among other organizations in a society—they must possess certain internal features. The presence of a formal division of labor, trained professionals, and fixed policies and procedures determine a group's organizational capacity. Organizational capacity is the element that allows a group to effectively compete with other groups in its orbit.

This chapter argues that micro-level intra-organizational dynamics determine organizational capacity and thus influence mezzo-level interactions that occur within *organizational fields,* a term used to describe a community of organizations.[1] To better understand the inter-organizational dynamics discussed in the following chapter, it is necessary to first examine the presence or absence of a formal division of labor, trained professionals, and fixed policies and procedures among the Comité, the UFW, and the Coastal Berry Company. As this chapter illustrates, of these three, the Comité was the least developed organizationally; this fact had a direct impact on its ability to affect other organizations and influence the course of the strawberry campaign.

An Office, a Phone, and a P.O. Box

In 2000 I had a series of encounters with Enrique Leal and the Comité that highlighted the difficulties encountered by the group as it tried to become a formal organization. Much had changed since the state agricultural labor relations board ruled that the workers' committee would be the bargaining agent for Coastal Berry's operations in the Watsonville area. Eddie and Jose Guadalupe Fernández were no longer involved with the Comité. Enrique Leal asserted that he had to let them go because "they were only in it for the money" (November 2000). According to Eddie Hernández's version of events, he had been pushed out of the group by Enrique Leal and others. He complained that the group had refused to reimburse him for various business-related expenses that he had paid out of his own pocket. In the fall of 2000 Eddie Hernández started leasing several acres of land to prepare for his own berry crop. He appeared upset about his experience with the Comité and expressed a desire to put it behind him. At this time the Comité also had a new lawyer. Jim Gumberg, who had been working pro bono, could no longer offer his services, and the group had to find another lawyer to help establish the union and negotiate a contract. In the summer of 2000 it started working with Jim Lorenz, a highly competent and controversial lawyer from Berkeley.[2]

One day that summer, I paid a visit to the group's recently opened office in a multi-story commercial building in downtown Watsonville for a meeting with Enrique Leal. The first floor of the building housed retail shops. The upper floors were occupied by service-oriented businesses including lawyers, accountants, and now a labor union. I had some difficulty finding the right office because there were no external markings on the door to indicate that the Comité was housed there. I hesitantly opened the door to what looked like a small reception area; this area was in fact the entire office. The room was furnished with a large new desk. On a long folding table of the sort used at church picnics were a variety of office machines, some still in boxes. I noticed a fax machine and a small copier on the table. Beside them were instruction manuals. Three chairs were arranged facing each other in front of the desk. The walls were almost completely bare. When I asked the secretary, Maria Teresa Cobo, whether Sergio Leal was in, she replied that she was not expecting him. I made casual conversation with her, letting her know the reason for my visit. She told me that she would be very interested in speaking with me further, "but not here." Sergio did not arrive, and I eventually left after arranging to interview Cobo another time.

I interviewed her a few days later to get her perspective on the new organization. The Comité secretary was a middle-aged woman originally from Guadalajara, Mexico, where she was employed in the offices of a large multinational corporation (*"una multinacional"*). She had been in the United States for eleven years. During that time she had worked as an accountant at a small Mexican-owned business. She had also been a secretary at the regional UFW office in Watsonville. In her view she had been dismissed from the UFW job in an unkind manner after a long illness. She had been with the Comité for about a month.

Maria Teresa Cobo's skills and experience as an administrative worker at the local office of a large farm labor union made her an attractive and probably rare candidate for the fledgling union. However, Cobo let me know that her responsibilities working for the Comité had not been made clear to her. She had originally been hired part-time to take phone calls. But her responsibilities quickly expanded from answering telephones to coordinating meetings, taking and filing worker grievances, and a great deal of translation work. Translation took a lot of time because all documents needed to be in a proper Spanish format: *"Debe ser en un buen español, no mocho* (It should be a proper Spanish, not informal)." She felt that the time-consuming work and her ability to translate professional English into professional Spanish were worthy of a raise. She also asserted that an actual office was a step in the right direction for the organization, *"para que la gente tenga donde ir a reclamar* (so that people would have somewhere to go and press claims)." Maria Teresa Cobo was well aware of the sort of work performed by effective unions, but she faced obstacles as she tried to perform this work for the nascent Comité.

Maria Teresa Cobo thought that having an office would lessen some problems with UFW supporters, who felt harassed and threatened in the fields. She supported the Comité's mission because, she said, if they could keep from becoming corrupt like other unions, they could do good things for workers at the company. At the same time, she seemed exasperated with the group. She complained that Sergio Leal was not a particularly competent administrator and leader and that the rest of the group's board members were not much better. From her perspective, it was imperative that the board members read, understand, and effectively explain the terms of the contract to workers in all the company's crews, especially those who still wanted UFW representation. She doubted that they were willing and able to do so.

Several weeks after my interview with Maria Teresa Cobo, I attended one of the Comité's meetings in the Watsonville office. This time, Sergio Leal, now president, and most of the board were present, as were Maria Teresa Cobo and Jim Lorenz. Extra folding chairs were arranged in a circle to accommodate all the attendees. Maria Teresa Cobo passed around the three-page agenda in Spanish. Jim Lorenz asked whether an English-language copy was available. When Maria Teresa Cobo responded in the negative, he asked whether one could be made available at the next meeting. Lorenz then opened the meeting and served as moderator. The first item concerned a press conference to be held by the group. "Who's gonna call the meeting?" Leal asked. "You are, baby—you're the president!" responded Lorenz.

It appeared that Sergio Leal had come directly from work to the evening meeting. His worn coveralls were grimy, and his hands were caked with dust. The next item of business concerned nineteen employees who had failed to return cards authorizing a 1-percent pay deduction for union dues. Since a contract could not be ratified until all employees were members of the union, and all employees had to agree to the deduction, it was important that these nineteen cards be submitted.[3] This topic started the group on an animated conversation about pro-UFW holdouts still upset with the Comité. Board members complained bitterly that these people were impeding progress at the company. Lorenz attempted to steer the conversation back to the items on the agenda.

That night, the Comité discussed several important items of business: the establishment of a grievance procedure, the creation of a hiring hall, and the implementation of a system of promotion and demotion for company workers. Lorenz also reminded board members that personal phone calls on the union cell phone were not allowed. At one point in the meeting, the group celebrated the opening of a commercial account at the local Wells Fargo Bank. The newly arrived checkbook was passed around the circle for everyone to see. However, Maria Teresa Cobo cautioned that since Coastal Berry had not yet begun depositing union dues, the Comité did not actually have money in the account.

The group also discussed hours and compensation for Maria Teresa Cobo, the secretary. At issue was whether she would be a full-time employee or work for the Comité only on a part-time contractual basis. Maria Teresa Cobo was actively participating in the conversation while simultaneously taking the minutes of the meeting. She recommended that she be hired full time and be paid more than she was currently earning. When asked whether he agreed with a proposal that she be paid the average local compensation for a secretary, a quiet member of the board responded that he did not know what secretaries earned in the area. Sergio Leal agreed that he did not know either, but "*Yo prefiero tenerla a ella que sabe de leyes* (I prefer to have her that knows about the laws)." "*Va a ver muchísimo dinero* (There's going to be a lot of money)," Maria Teresa Cobo assured the Comité members. The meeting adjourned with little progress on this or the other items on the agenda. A few months later, Maria Teresa Cobo was no longer with the Comité. "She turned out to be a real nightmare," Lorenz later told me. He said that she had continued to press for greater compensation, but would only communicate about it to Sergio Leal.

Losing Maria Teresa Cobo was just one indication of the Comité's lack of organizational capacity; the group failed to formalize itself on a number of fronts. It had put itself on the right path by hiring professional administrative staff and legal counsel, but it was unable to make effective use of this staff because it was still operating as a loosely organized group of individuals without a formal division of labor that included departments with official duties and responsibilities. For example, Eddie Hernández should not have been paying for business-related expenses out of his own pocket; this is not the way that formally established organizations operate. The group also lacked a formal set of policies and procedures necessary for performing the day-to-day functions of the organization; Maria Teresa Cobo's frustration over her vague yet ever-expanding job duties points to the lack of clarity in the group's division of labor and responsibilities. In the end, Sergio Leal and the rest of the board were fieldworkers, not administrators. One embittered UFW supporter even refused to call them a union. In an interview, Juan Corona stated, "*No le puedo llamar yo sindicato, no se ni como llamarle porque no hacen ningún tipo de representación* (I can't call it a union. I don't know what to call them because they don't provide any type of representation) [October 2000]. Corona's statement makes it evident that the group was not functioning as it should have been. The Comité was clearly not yet a formal organization.

Dissent in Organizational Society

To compete as a labor union in an advanced industrial democratic society, the Comité, like the UFW before it, was forced to comply with certain organizational imperatives such as a formal division of labor and written policies and procedures to guide the operation. The Comité and its supporters had not envisioned these requirements when they originally sought to oust the UFW from Coastal Berry. Enrique Leal repeatedly told me, "*No mas queremos trabajar en paz* (We only want to work in peace)." But ousting the UFW meant developing an organizational infrastructure capable of engaging with other established organizations including state agencies, civic groups, and for-profit entities. The Comité was never able to fully develop this capacity.

Although immigrant networks held sway in the fields, organizations, not social networks, ultimately determined the outcome of events at Coastal Berry. Many organizations (including the ALRB, discussed in the following chapter) were involved in the campaign. However, the underdeveloped Comité, the UFW, and Coastal Berry were the dominant actors that determined the fate of Central Coast strawberry workers between 1996 and 2003. Organizations are social technologies created to accomplish particular tasks. Their effectiveness in achieving these tasks is based on leadership, formal division of labor, and trained professionals; these factors allow them to influence other organizations. An organizational approach is therefore necessary to understand what happened during the UFW campaign.

The sociologist Max Weber recognized the importance of bureaucratically organized groups beginning with the earliest stages of the modern era. He wrote, "The decisive reason for the advance of bureaucratic organization has always been its purely technical superiority over any former organization. The fully developed bureaucratic mechanism compares with other organizations exactly as does the machine with non-mechanical modes of production" (Gerth and Mills 1946: 214). Although he was ambivalent about the virtues of bureaucratic organization due to their depersonalization, Weber saw their rise as inevitable. Bureaucratization, according to Weber, was increasing in the world. As he predicted, formal organizations have come to dominate modern societies. Today, this structural template is seen in groups across the state, market, and civil society. Charles

Perrow, a contemporary theorist of organizations, calls ours an organizational society. Perrow is referring to the fact that it is hard to find an element of contemporary life not directly affected by organizations, whether public or private, religious or secular, for profit or not.

Weber tells us that bureaucratic organizations are rational systems of supervision, management, and control. They are designed to coordinate the activities and responsibilities of officials and employees in these groupings toward some specified end or goal. Weber characterized bureaucracies as governed by several principles (see Gerth and Mills 1946).[4] Three of them are relevant to my analysis of the UFW and the Coastal Berry campaign:

Leadership

The German concept of *Herrschaft* that Weber employed in his discussions of leadership varies slightly from modern American English ideas of leadership. *Herrschaft* has been translated as "imperative control" or "imperative co-ordination" (see Gerth and Mills 1946). This conceptualization of leadership emphasizes authority relations and the legitimacy of authority within organizations. The issue of legitimacy is especially important in Weber's thinking. He wants to know on what basis people accept the authority of those in power within an organization. He arrives at three possibilities:

- *Traditional authority* is rooted in convention. Obedience and authority under this type of leadership are based on personal relationships to people in power.
- *Charismatic authority* springs from devotion to those rare individuals who have the ability to command a following due to their personal characteristics. Examples include Mahatma Gandhi and Dr. Martin Luther King Jr.
- *Legal rational authority* is based on formal rules and procedures. This type of authority makes use of a bureaucratic administrative staff and is the basis of authority in modern organizations.

For Weber traditional authority was becoming increasingly less common in the modern world because of its inefficiency. Charismatic authority was unstable due to its dependence on a singular personality. This made legal rational authority ascendant in the modern era as organizational structures became increasingly formalized.

Formal Division of Labor

Formal organizations operate as hierarchies with a stable system of superordination and subordination. Official duties in an organization are distributed in a fixed manner to officials qualified to fulfill the tasks assigned to their particular office. In the modern organization this means that the accounting department works on a specified set of tasks that are different from the tasks assigned to marketing or sales, for example. At a college or university, the work of the registrar is quite different from that of the bursar, and so forth.

Trained Professionals

Officials in modern organizations are often professionals who have undergone training, passed examinations, and or have requisite diplomas or certificates that qualify them for certain positions. Weber writes, "More and more, the specialized knowledge of the expert became the foundation for the power position of the office holder" (Gerth and Mills 1946: 235).

Social movement scholars have expanded on Weber's organizational imperatives in their discussions of collective action and social change. Researchers in this area have determined that for individuals to successfully effect social change within an institutional setting, they must do so in a manner that is coordinated and sustained, which requires social movement groups to exhibit at least a minimal degree of organizational capacity. In the sections that follow I assess the organizational capacities of the Comité, the UFW, and Coastal Berry using Weber's three organizational characteristics described above.

The Comité's Emergence and Attempt to Formalize

The Comité first emerged as a bona fide legal entity when it requested a state-sanctioned election at the Coastal Berry Company. The documentation submitted to the ALRB's office in Salinas on July 16, 1998, was the first formal mention of the Coastal Berry Farmworkers Committee. Jose Guadalupe Fernández was the sole representative of the Labor Organization Petitioner on the bilingual ALRB State of California Petition for Certification form. A single address was listed for both petitioner and representative: a post office box in Watsonville belonging to Jose G. Fernández, a truck driver at Coastal Berry. Guadalupe Fernández, as he was known among his coworkers, was a young man aged 22 when he submitted the petition to the state authorities.

Two weeks prior, on the night of July 1, local television viewers on the Central Coast of California saw Fernández struggling with county sheriffs and State Highway Patrol officers after a melee at a Coastal Berry facility, discussed in Chapter 3. After being detained for several hours, Fernández was released without being charged with a crime. The event was nevertheless often mentioned in the press when he was named head of the Coastal Berry Farmworkers Committee. As a result of his detainment, Fernández was dismissed from the company, and thereafter he limited his involvement in the Comité. When asked about the formation of the Comité and its initial members, another of the group's founders, Eddie Hernández, told me the following: "When the group was initially formed, it was only three of us in the struggle, Francisco Gudiño, Sergio Leal, and me." He continued, "Later, as this began to take shape, Guadalupe Fernández emerged as president of the Comité because he knew both languages" (July 2000).

Sergio Leal emerged as spokesperson and initial president of the Comité after Fernández was fired. Eddie Hernández was articulate, knowledgeable, and well-spoken in his native Spanish. He had a detailed understanding of the political and corporate machinations that had given rise to the current stalemate between capital interests and organized labor.[5] Yet, he did not speak English, nor was it certain that he possessed legal immigration status in United States. Thus, Sergio Leal became the president of the Comité by default.

A year later, now deemed a labor organization by the state, the Comité was required to submit a Labor Organization Information Report (known as form LM-1) to the US Department of Labor.[6] Fernández's name was absent from the document. Instead, seven people are mentioned as the organization's officers in the Comité's 1999 LM-1 filings. The names included Sergio Leal as president, four vice presidents, a recording secretary, and a secretary-treasurer. Of the seven initial members of the board of directors indicated on the form, two vice-presidents have their signature written by others with a handwritten note in Spanish beginning in part, "*Firma autorizada por [X] a [Y]*," meaning that person X had authorized person Y to sign on his or her behalf.

Several notable changes had occurred in the Comité leadership by the following winter. Jose Guadalupe Fernández remained uninvolved. However, three of the officers mentioned in the 1999 LM-1 report— Eddie Hernández, Felipe Ruiz, and Francisco Gudiño—were also conspicuously absent from the leadership of the organization. According to Sergio Leal, Hernández and Gudiño "were in it only for the money" (November 2000). Eddie Hernández's wife saw it differently. "After so many late nights, after so many struggles for so many things that we want for the people ... it's hard to know that other persons take control and say, 'we are the Comité.'" She chided Hernández for not mentioning the numerous personal expenses for office supplies, faxes, and mass mailings they had funded with their own money, which the Comité refused to reimburse. Hernández responded coolly, "*Yo no estoy afuera* (I am not out [of the group])." Eddie Hernández's movement into and out of a leadership role, the loss of Maria Teresa Cobo, and Jose Guadalupe Fernández's refusal to participate together show that the Comité lacked clear and stable leadership, an essential organizational trait identified by Weber. These changes had significant implications for the group as it became increasingly responsible for the work of a labor union.

During another interview Eddie Hernández described the initial emergence of the Comité as a "metamorphosis." This was an apt description of the fledgling organization. The farm workers who took it upon themselves to challenge the UFW in the fields were not as effective when it came to the technical details of labor law and organizational management. In the power struggles and personnel changes among top officers can be found a violation of Weber's principles of rational bureaucratic organizations. Constant changes among the Comité's top officers challenged the legitimacy of its leadership among workers, particularly those who still pined for the UFW. Although Sergio Leal's English abilities may have helped him to communicate with groups and individuals beyond the fields who did not speak Spanish, he was a reluctant and often frustrated president of the union.

The Comité clearly lacked a formal division of labor and paid professional staffers characteristic of complex organizations. After the 1998 election, a great deal of the organizational maintenance work apparently was done by employees such as Maria Teresa Cobo or lawyers. The Comité's first lawyer, Jim Gumberg, spoke with frustration about having to double as press agent for the organization. "Yeah, [UFW spokesperson] Marc Grossman was constantly pounding out press releases, and we never did that. I did one myself once, just because I couldn't take all the calls and I wanted to make sure we got heard" (November 2000). However, it was difficult for Gumberg to handle public relations matters (in which he had no training) along with the legal aspects of the case. He was not working exclusively for the

Comité, nor was he receiving payment for his work, so he could devote only limited time and energy to the group.

The Comité was further hampered in its abilities to establish formal policies and procedures because while it was formally recognized as a labor organization, it was not authorized to act as a bargaining agent. The Comité stated as much in an attachment to the 1999 LM-1 form, in which it wrote,

> Though the Committee has one [*sic*] three straight elections at the Coastal Berry Company, it has yet to be certified by the California Agricultural Labor Relations Board ("ALRB"). Accordingly, the company in which the elections were won, Coastal Berry Company, has steadfastly refused to enter into collective bargaining with the Committee, and has continued to refuse to do so until such time as the Committee is certified as the bargaining representative by the ALRB. (Attachment 1 Form LM-1)

The statement continues by saying that general practices and procedures such as authorizing bargaining demands, ratifying contract terms, authorizing strikes, and issuing work permits would be determined after certification. Without certification the Comité was in limbo. It was nominally a labor organization, but without certification it could not begin the work of a union.

The Comité had neither the intention nor the ability to function as a conventional labor union. When asked about the group's original goals, Eddie Hernández responded with a wry grin: "Look, the real truth, the real truth, the first goal was to get the union [UFW] to stop bothering us" (July 2000). Others expressed similar disdain toward the UFW. "They're outsiders coming into the fields and trying to be your friend," said a Coastal Berry worker in reference to organizers, "and they insult us when we don't support the union" (Linneman 1997). It was frustrations such as this that led workers to seek the riddance of the UFW. However, the Comité lacked a clear platform, and because it was not certified, it was unable to implement formal policies and procedures. The group also suffered from limited to nonexistent organizational infrastructure. It had no fixed offices with formally trained officials occupying those offices. When the Comité was finally certified as bargaining agent, its leaders struggled to perform the duties required of them as union managers. The Comité thus found itself constantly responding to the actions of other groups in the organizational milieu of the campaign. Its defensive and reactionary approach attests to its inchoate nature and differed markedly from the behavior of the more organizationally sophisticated UFW.

The UFW

The UFW is much more representative of Weberian principles of bureaucratic organizations than is the Comité. The organizational formalization and adaptation of institutional practices assumed by the UFW in its early years are the mechanisms that allowed it to eventually overcome the Comité's challenges. The UFW employed multiple public, political, and legal strategies to unionize the industry and Coastal Berry. This approach required a complex organization with specialized offices tasked with creating, coordinating, and executing its multiple strategies. The Comité was never able to develop a similar organizational structure or practices. Despite the strength of individual ties in the workforce, the enduring and therefore dominant social structure of the campaign proved to be the complex, formal organization. Interactions among organizations and the ability of organizations to manipulate those interactions resulted in the eventual outcome of the campaign in favor of the UFW. The union's masterful ability to navigate its organizational orbit can be traced to its organizational structure, which has proven remarkably resilient over its forty-year history and can be credited for its continued existence, especially after the death of Cesar Chavez.

The UFW's 1996 convention was an occasion for celebration. Even though long-time, revered leader Cesar Chavez had passed away in 1993, with his son-in-law Arturo Rodriguez at the helm the organization had embarked on an aggressive organizing campaign. By the time of the September meeting, the UFW could boast of thirteen straight election victories, including contract ratification with the Chateau St. Michelle winery in Washington State. Still, attempting to organize workers at California's largest strawberry producer was a major undertaking. If the union were successful, however, it would vastly expand union membership and reestablish the UFW's prominence as the state's premier farm labor organization. The union's new president seemed ready for the challenge.

Rodriguez had recently been named vice president of the AFL-CIO and had been appointed a member of its executive council. AFL-CIO president John Sweeney joined US Secretary of Housing and Urban Development chief Henry Cisneros to speak at the UFW's September meeting in Fresno. The fact that two nationally prominent speakers addressed the UFW convention was not unusual and speaks to the clout of the union in labor and political circles.

Both Cisneros and Sweeney gave rousing speeches to a crowd estimated at 2,000 people. Cisneros delivered his message entirely in Spanish. He urged eligible immigrants to obtain citizenship and vote so that they might have a voice in the country's political process. Sweeney spoke about the continued need for workers across the country to organize. He pledged to participants that the country's estimated 13 million unionized workers stood behind the UFW's efforts to organize the Central Coast strawberry workers. Both speeches were well received by workers (McCarthy 1996).

The UFW's most important affairs are conducted at its convention according to its constitution, which was amended that year in Fresno. The convention is a biennial event at which union leadership and members come together; it is usually held in Fresno though it does change location occasionally. At the convention voting delegates have the power to establish new policies, interpret or amend by-laws of the union's constitution, and elect officers. According to the UFW's constitution, "The Supreme Authority of the Union shall reside in Convention. In Convention assembled, the Union shall have the plenary power to achieve, regulate, and direct the objects, policies, affairs, organization, and administration of the union, and power shall be legislative, executive, and judicial" (UFW constitution: 2). It is at the national convention that delegates from all union chapters convene, exchange information, and elect officers.

The convention is a festive affair, with union delegates from all over the country waving red flags and listening to major speakers. During the 2000 convention, then-Senator Hillary Clinton spoke. As one retired 80-year-old farmworker said of the convention, it is "a real democratic event.... You don't hear lies here. This isn't like a political convention for the Republicans or the Democrats. It's farm workers deciding who the leaders should be and what the policies should be" (Maxwell 2000).[7]

Beginning in 1984, the convention began to elect seven national officers: a president, a secretary-treasurer, three vice presidents, and two national vice presidents. National officers usually serve four-year terms. These seven positions constitute the union's executive board. The union also has an executive committee comprising the president, secretary-treasurer, and three vice presidents but not the two national vice presidents. Between conventions the affairs of the union are conducted by the executive board and the executive committee. The executive board meets at least once every ninety days. Between board meetings the executive committee is the highest authority in the union. At committee meetings, quorum can be reached by three members provided that the president and secretary-treasurer are present. The UFW constitution does not, however, clearly specify executive committee responsibilities as it does those of the board. According to the constitution, "In order to promote and conserve the welfare and interest of the Union, it shall have the power to take such action as in its opinion it may deem necessary and beneficial to carry out the objects and purposes of this union" (UFW constitution, Article 39 Section E). This includes the "power of the purse" along with all other tasks that ensure the proper functioning of a complex organization.

One important task of the board and ultimately the president is the creation and funding of administrative departments and offices (Article 43). Some of the departments mentioned in the constitution are Organizing, Boycott, Strike, Legal, Negotiations, Research, and Membership. In actuality, the specialized departments tasked with coordinating the work of the union are the Public Action, Organizing, Communications, and Accounting departments. The UFW also has fourteen Public Action offices throughout the United States, a recruiting office in Los Angeles, and a second national office in Washington, D.C.

The UFW's 84-page constitution describes a highly complex set of policies and procedures. These formal practices carefully govern the conduct of the organization, its officers, and its various departments and offices. These policies and procedures form the basis of the UFW's organizational capacity, which allowed it to effectively negotiate the organizational environment during the strawberry campaign. Although the union exhibited a complex organizational structure, however, there was a gap between the UFW as constituted and the UFW as manifested. As Perrow (1986) concludes, organizations never fully bureaucratize.

Contrary to the aforementioned comments of the retired farmworker, a review of the UFWs LM-2 files demonstrates that the union is not an especially democratic or grassroots organization, particularly in its leadership. In its forty-six years of existence it has had two presidents. From its founding in 1968 until 1993, that president was Cesar Chavez. From Chavez's death to the present, Arturo Rodriguez has been president. The executive board is only slightly more fluid. From 1996 to the present, Irv Hirshenbaum has served as first vice president. Since 2000 Efren Barajas has been second vice president. This evidence suggests that the UFW has succumbed to what the sociologist Robert Michels (1911) famously refers to as the Iron Law of Oligarchy. While studying German labor unions, Michels noticed a phenomenon whereby the top leadership of large labor organizations ossifies, with directors remaining at top posts for extended periods. Similarly, Perrow writes that the top of many organizational structures is never fully bureaucratized. Power tends to become concentrated in the upper tiers of the hierarchy where decision making does not always follow standardized policies and procedures, even if the lower rungs of the organization do function according to standardized protocols.

Concentration of power and deviation from written rules at the upper echelons of an otherwise bureaucratized organization certainly seem to be the case with the UFW. This had concrete implications for the strawberry campaign. According to several campaign field organizers I interviewed, the campaign was a markedly top-down affair, with the union's executive board holding the reins. One stated, "Artie Rodriguez was there and obviously he was in charge.... So when Artie was there, the structure would evolve into him and members of the E-board [executive board]. They just like to have all their big leaders together" (Jessica Lara, October 2000). This top-down, nondemocratic structure partially explains the UFW's difficulties in the fields.

In August 2000, around the same time that I observed a Comité meeting, I paid a visit to the UFW regional office in Watsonville to meet with vice president Efren Barajas, in charge of the Watsonville area. The UFW office was in a downtown office building named "La Manzana" (the Apple). The building sat on a street corner, and its outside walls were painted with beautiful Mexican American–themed murals. To reach the UFW offices required walking through a pleasant courtyard and up an interior set of stairs. As I entered I could hear slow, mournful Mexican music playing at low volume on a radio. Inside the spacious reception areas were two shrines on opposite walls. Atop a rustic wooden box painted white was an altar to the Virgen de Guadalupe, adorned with burning candles and fresh flowers. On the opposite wall was a photo of Cesar Chavez adorned with crucifixes. Only a few people were in the office, and it seemed quieter than what I imagined it must have been like during the height of the campaign. By this time, the campaign in the fields was winding down, and UFW strategy was focused in the courtroom.

The massive task of organizing 20,000 workers required an organizational infrastructure flexible enough to accommodate rapid expansion without the loss of control due to sudden expansion. The UFW succeeded in this. The union employed 32 people in 1995 according to LM-2 reports. That number increased significantly the next year to 53 and then nearly doubled to 104 in 1997. At the height of the campaign in 1998, the union employed 120 workers, including dozens of organizers as well as researchers, accountants, service representatives, and public-relations officers. By the time I interviewed Barajas in 2000, the employee count had subsided to 81.[8] The union's organizational infrastructure and rigid leadership allowed it to expand and contract rapidly to deal with the shifting demands of the campaign. This flexibility permitted the union to rapidly mobilize and precisely deploy necessary resources in a general or concerted and focused manner. No such efforts would have been possible without strong leadership; a complex division of offices, including legal and public relations departments; and formal policies and procedures to govern the conduct of its officials.

Coastal Berry

The Coastal Berry Company also exhibited strong leadership, a complex division of labor, and formal policies and procedures. However, a change in the company's ownership early in the campaign triggered unforeseen shifts in the organization's authority relations, which proved detrimental to the UFW's mobilization campaign. This outcome is instructive because it demonstrates how informal social networks can operate, both positively and negatively, within an organization's formal division of labor. Coastal Berry also provides other lessons on the function of organizations. Its internal changes give us insight on the resiliency of formal organizational structures. As the focus of a unionization campaign, Coastal Berry was under a tremendous amount of pressure from 1997 to 2000. This pressure affected the organization's ability to meet its objectives. Unlike the Comité and the UFW, Coastal Berry is a market-oriented, for-profit entity. Its primary function is to generate profits for its owners. The extended unionization campaign hampered the company's profitability. Yet the company was able to adjust accordingly and continue producing berries (if not always profitably) during the unionization campaign and subsequent organizational changes. The fact that it could do so can be traced to its effective implementation of Weberian organizational imperatives of leadership, formal division of labor, and established policies and procedures. Despite changes in personnel and authority relations, the fundamental nature of the organization remained the same.

Organizations, the sociologist Charles Perrow tells us, are tools.[9] They are created by their masters to perform certain functions. In the case of Coastal Berry, the function was profit making. Unlike most other berry-growing operations in the region, Coastal Berry was never a small or family-owned operation. Its size made it anomalous in the local industry. The company came into existence in 1982 as a collaborative effort between Dick Telles, a local farmer, and Gargiulo, a large produce company based in Naples, Florida, that operated extensive acreage in California. In the mid-1990s, Gargiulo was the largest packer and shipper of tomatoes in the country, with revenues over USD 100 million annually (Fisher 1995). For the first decade of its existence, Coastal

Berry was operated by Telles and produced tomatoes as a semi-autonomous division of Gargiulo, a national produce company.

In 1993 Monsanto, the huge agrochemical company based in St. Louis, acquired a 49.9 percent share of Gargiulo with an option to buy the entire company at a later date. According to industry observers, Monsanto was eager to make this purchase because it wanted to expand its presence in agricultural biotechnology (Fisher 1995). This claim was given credence in 1996, when Monsanto acquired a 49.9 percent share of Calgene, a company that had successfully developed genetically engineered tomatoes. As part of the $30 million deal, Monsanto ceded control of Gargiulo to Calgene. The following year, Monsanto completed its purchase of Calgene and regained control of Coastal Berry as a division of Gargiulo. When targeted by the UFW as part of the union's corporate strategy, Monsanto agreed to sell Gargiulo's Coastal Berry Company to two pro-union investors. According to a Monsanto spokesperson, "We determined that this was not a strategic fit with Monsanto's other businesses" (Baldwin Hick and Steyer 1997). One of the investors would sell his share of the company to the other less than a year after they purchased it jointly. In 2004 David Gladstone, the remaining pro-union investor, sold Coastal Berry to the Dole Food Company. Similar to the berries it produced, Coastal Berry had become a commodity. With the possible exception of the 1997 acquisition by Butler and Gladstone, it had been bought and sold multiple times with the purpose of generating capital gains for its owners.

As a subsidiary of a large corporation, Coastal Berry did not operate under the same financial constraints as the other small-scale producers in the region. Furthermore, despite its large size, day-to-day operations at the Coastal Berry Company were conducted with minimal corporate oversight. Larry Galper was the general manager when the company was sold in 1997. Galper had worked for Coastal Berry since its inception in 1982. Because Gargiulo was based in Florida and focused on tomatoes, Galper had considerable independence in the operation of the Central California berry subsidiary. During this time the company was divided into two divisions, inland and coastal—the former closer to the Pacific Coast, the latter inland in the Pajaro Valley. Each division in turn comprised several worksites known as ranches. The inland division included the San Andres, Jensen, and Salinas ranches. The coastal division comprised the Riverside ranch, which actually consisted of several different worksites. Aside from the different areas they farmed, each division had its own work crews, foremen, and supervisors. The two divisions operated mostly autonomously though both ultimately reported to Galper. Their independence shaped the outcome of the strawberry campaign.

During Galper's long tenure at the Coastal Berry Company, he exercised a management style that may be described as classic *patrón* with a strong and heavily involved leadership. Former employees tell stories of Galper periodically taking the office staff into the fields to pick strawberries for a day to remind them of the importance of pickers to the overall operation. Such behavior engendered a mutual sense of respect between Galper and many workers. One worker told me, "*Lorenzo no era el tipo de persona que te decía, 'haz esto,' o, 'haz aquello.' Él se salía de su pick up y te enseñaba como hacerlo* (Lorenzo wasn't the type of guy who would tell you 'Do this,' 'Do that.' He would get out of his pick-up and would show you how to do it)" (October 2000).[10] Many (though not all) workers I interviewed spoke positively about Galper's management style, which they felt brought everyone in the company together. Certainly, the company was profitable while he was at the helm. It was a useful tool for its masters, as Perrow might say.

The 1997 sale of Coastal Berry to David Gladstone and Landon Butler resulted in major changes to the organizational dynamic within the company. Galper and several other high-level managers were dismissed. Employing an out-of-state search firm, the new owners recruited David Smith from Visalia in the Central Valley to be the company's new president.[11] Following the sale, Smith and the new management team were unable to sustain the level of organizational cohesion that prevailed during Galper's tenure. To be sure, some workers would certainly not have described the company as anything resembling one big happy family, but the sale and subsequent change in leadership accelerated the deterioration of worker-management relations that had previously been ameliorated by a strong degree of vertical integration. Smith remained in the top position for less than a year.

The lack of cohesion and strong leadership at a time of tremendous pressure from a unionization campaign severely strained the intra-organizational dynamic at Coastal Berry. Under the new leadership regime, the differences between the two divisions were exacerbated, and interaction among the various strata of personnel decreased. It was in this environment that the power of the Leal family network at the inland division became even more apparent. As mid-level managers and supervisors began to see their control over hiring, firing, and promotion threatened with the possibility of a union hiring hall, they began to pressure and intimidate pro-UFW workers. According to one UFW supporter,

O sea que ya empezaron a, o sea ya le daban a uno más carilla los mayordomos, más cuando miraban que se ponía una gorra o botón. O sea que era él a quien debían seguir. Luego trataban de intimidarlo, o la ponchadora agarrarle cajas y cajas para que les metan tiquetes a uno. (The foremen started to hassle us. More so when they saw one put on a [UFW] button or cap. Later, they would try to intimidate one, or the puncher would pick on one's boxes so that we would get a warning). [October 2000]

For reasons explained below, these workers lacked recourse to company authorities above mid-level managers. Whereas previously there existed a high degree of cohesion in the company, after the sale workers' experiences were more determined by the narrow occupational units to which they belonged.

This reduction in interaction severely curtailed access to information that would normally be available to workers via formal channels of communication. Under normal circumstances the lack of dialogue between crews in different divisions was not significant. During the unionization campaign, however, the ability to share information became critical. Lack of information and misinformation in the form of rumors spread via personal networks were rampant among the crews during the campaign. In this tumultuous time, it is striking to note how little pickers actually knew about Coastal Berry affairs beyond their immediate work environments. Many did not know who the president was or who among the other crews was involved in the anti-UFW movement. Such crucial information would have been important to workers in deciding which courses of action best suited them. As workers turned to family and kin during uncertain times, the power of informal social networks increased and the dissemination of information via official channels of communication within the formal division of labor began to deteriorate.

An increasing insularity also emerged in the company's management team. The dismissal of Galper and other well-known high-level managers at the company was widely viewed as a political move. Many in the company's professional staff believed that these people had been dismissed because of their alleged anti-UFW positions. Their replacements were wary of involving themselves unnecessarily with workers in the fields, lest they meet the same fate as those previously dismissed. They performed their jobs but shied away from becoming too occupied with labor politics. Consequently, they had very little interaction with workers. The decreased level of interaction traversing different levels of company personnel further eroded the bonds of reciprocal engagement among different categories of workers.

It was in this tumultuous environment that mid-level managers came to assume an inordinate amount of power at the company. Like the *caciques* discussed in the previous chapter, these individuals took advantage of a chaotic and disruptive situation to suit their own interests. In their detached approach to worker issues, the upper strata of company management relegated much of the daily operations in the fields to mid-level supervisors and foremen. It would have been difficult for these recently hired upper-level managers to assume much responsibility in the fields anyway because they were new to the company. Interacting with workers became almost exclusively the domain of mid-level managers, who seized the opportunity and took it upon themselves to consolidate as much power as possible. Based on conversations with employees at multiple levels of the organizational hierarchy, it seems that executives at company headquarters were unaware that this was happening. Even if they had known about it, it is unlikely they would have been able to respond without jeopardizing their own positions.

Profit-oriented companies are commonly bought and sold several times over the course of their existence. The changes in leadership that sometimes result from acquisitions, however, can have an impact on the structure of the organization, including changes in managerial personnel and management style. That is exactly what happened at Coastal Berry Company before, during, and after the UFW's efforts to organize workers there. Mid-level managers were quick to take advantage of the power vacuum left in the wake of Galper's departure. It was thought that the sale of the company to pro-union investors would minimize anti-UFW sentiment. Ironically, Galper's departure probably exacerbated those tensions: a crisis in leadership led to the usurpation of power and authority by managers in the middle levels of an otherwise well-organized company. Most striking is that Coastal Berry continued to function successfully as an organization in spite of its tumultuous history and management turnover. This outcome is a clear example of what Weber characterizes as the "permanent character of the bureaucratic machine." This notion refers to the way in which, once established, organizational structures tend to endure, regardless of the specific personnel occupying the various offices of the organization. Weber would say that organizations persist where individuals do not. The brief history of interactions among the Coastal Berry Company, the Comité, and the UFW would seem to confirm this.

Struggling to Bureaucratize

When I first met Sergio Leal, the Comité president, in 2000, he offered to give me a tour of Watsonville. He picked me up at the central plaza in a rusted old Geo metro. He explained that the door was broken, and from the driver's side, he pulled on a rope tied to a lever that disengaged the locking mechanism on the passenger-side door. Grinning, he then asked me to open the door, which easily swung open. I found the inside of the car to be messy and cluttered with unopened letters and documents strewn about. We then drove to various sites in the Pajaro Valley as he explained to me the history of the Comité. As we drove around, I couldn't help but think of Leal and his car as a metaphor to describe the organization.

Two years after it had first formed in 1998, the Comité was only beginning to open a bank account and exhibited few characteristics of a formal organization. It struggled to become fully bureaucratized during the entirety of its brief existence. Ultimately, it was clear that the group woefully underdeveloped as an organization to effectively compete against the UFW. Conversely, the more established UFW continuously demonstrated a robust organizational capacity as it approached the labor organizing effort on multiple fronts. It dominated the political, legal, and public dimensions of the campaign. Thus, even if a large number of workers at Coastal Berry were not ready to accept the UFW as their bargaining agent, the UFW's leadership, formal division of labor, and robust army of paid professionals performing specialized tasks enabled it to outmaneuver the Comité in an environment dominated by other complex organizations. There was no way that the Comité, a group of farmworker volunteers with limited experience with formal organizations, could hope to compete against the UFW. Meanwhile, the Coastal Berry Company had all of the attributes of a formal organization. This allowed it to successfully withstand a challenging period of transition and restructuring during the unionization campaign. What these three organizations demonstrate is that groups that manage to develop and sustain a bureaucratic form are better able to achieve their objectives compared with those that do not exhibit such characteristics.

The metric borrowed from Max Weber concerning leadership, formal division of labor, and trained professionals thus explains why some organizations succeed and others fail. Recall that Perrow (1986) describes organizations as tools; they are social technologies created to perform certain functions. For the Coastal Berry Company that function was the generation of profits; for the Comité, it was the ouster of the

UFW from Coastal Berry. The UFW's function was, and is, to be a collective bargaining agent for farmworkers. Regardless of function, as we have seen, all organizations, no matter how big or small, must conform to certain principles if they are to be successful in accomplishing whatever task has been set out for them. Coastal Berry and the UFW were formal organizations with identifiable leadership, a formal division of labor, and trained professionals. That is why they are still in existence today. The Comité never managed to fully bureaucratize, and that is why it ceased to exist. Because the Comité never bureaucratized, it was unable to develop the organizational capacity necessary to successfully compete against other organizations in an effort to achieve its goals. In an organizational society such as ours, structural changes are usually the result of interorganizational dynamics.

Learning the Rules of the Game

The fight to unionize the strawberry industry began in the fields but ended in the courts. There, the Agricultural Labor Relations Board interpreted labor law to adjudicate disputes between competing parties. The Agricultural Labor Relations Act (ALRA), an institution, was a major factor in the outcome. We can crudely though accurately enough describe institutions as the "rules of the game" that govern interorganizational dynamics.[12] Institutions emerge when organizations create formal and informal rules that govern their interactions. They influence organizational behavior even as they (the rules) are subject to change by organizations. In the agricultural industry these institutional arrangements usually take the form of legislation or policy regimes such as the ALRA that govern the conduct of producers, labor, and labor advocates. Understanding how these rules operate within particular organizational fields enables collective actors to pursue their interests with greater success than would otherwise be possible.

From this perspective, organizational capacity is the necessary precondition for gaining institutional knowledge and awareness, which are required for survival in any organizational field. Once organizations have acquired this knowledge and awareness, they are able to interact with other organizations in their field to create and manipulate institutional arrangements in society. For loosely organized individuals in marginalized groups such as the Comité, learning the rules of the game means adapting procedural norms and a repertoire of strategies that allows them to meet their objectives. This behavior is learned, applied, and rewarded within specific organizational fields. As this chapter demonstrates, the Comité was never able to develop sufficiently to fully learn the rules. It was thus unable to successfully compete against the UFW and other organizations.

In the next chapter I examine the role of the UFW's organizational capacity and institutional knowledge in its efforts to bring change to the California strawberry fields. Careful scrutiny and analysis of those events reveals a sophisticated organization with the institutional knowledge necessary to make it a dominant player in the state's courts and agricultural fields.

---

[1] A meso-level analysis dealing with interorganizational relations that occur within organizational fields follows in the next chapter.

[2] In 1966 Lorenz helped found the California Rural Legal Assistance (CRLA), a nonprofit legal assistance program for the state's rural poor. In the late 1990s Lorenz filed several suits against the UFW and was considered to be anti-union by many UFW supporters.

[3] For comparison, UFW membership dues are set at 2 percent for all unionized employees.

[4] According to Weber, bureaucratic organizations can be characterized by the following six principles: fixed and official jurisdictional areas; a fixed system of super- and subordination; proceedings are conducted on the basis of written documents; usually require training for specialized positions; when at work, employees will engage in the business of the organization; and the work of an office follows rules that can be learned (Gerth and Mills 1946: 196–198).

[5] In video footage of the July 16 altercation, Eddie Hernández can be heard exhorting his fellow workers, "*Con palabras, compañeros, con palabras* (Use words, friends, use words)."

[6] Unions with receipts in excess of $200,000 are required to submit LM-2 forms. This is what the UFW submits annually to the US Department of Labor. With annual receipts under $10,000, the Comité submitted LM-1s.

[7] This section draws from the Constitution of the United Farm Workers of America, AFL-CIO, adopted at the thirteenth Constitutional Convention in Fresno, California, August 31 and September 1, 1996. I have also reviewed the union's LM-2 forms, which all labor organizations with annual receipts over $200,000 are required to submit to the US Department of Labor annually.

[8] These numbers do not adequately represent all those involved in the campaign as there were AFL-CIO personnel who also participated on behalf of the UFW.

[9] Perrow says that organizations are "recalcitrant tools" (1986) because they don't always perform the way we would like them to.

[10] This former employee of Galper referred to him by his Mexican name, Lorenzo.

[11] The high-level supervisor at Coastal Berry who relayed this information to me emphasized the fact that the search firm did not specialize in agricultural production companies and that the firm was located in New York.

[12] The term *institution* can sometimes refer to discrete organizations. However, I employ a more specific conceptualization of the term derived from

economic sociology. See, for example, Powell and DiMaggio 1991; Fligstein 2002; and Scott 2008.

6

The Triumph of Effective Bureaucracy

An analysis of the California strawberry campaign from an organizational fields perspective reveals that the UFW used several institutional strategies that were key to its success in the campaign. First are *political and legal dimensions* associated with actions taken by the UFW to secure the support or at least the neutrality of the state, including politicians and government agencies at the local, state, and federal levels. These relationships became critical toward the end of the organizing drive, when the fight became litigious and moved from the fields into the courts. After these political dimensions, the second set of institutional strategies employed by the UFW during the organizing drive may be termed the *corporate campaign,* which refers to the union's strategy to extend the campaign against the industry beyond the immediate sites of production—taking the campaign out of the fields and into the public arena. That involved using industry research and financial analysis to determine how to best impede a company or industry's ability to remain profitable and in good standing with the general public, which would in turn render it more vulnerable to unionization. To this end the UFW employed aggressive tactics and the media in the same way that other unions such as the Service Employees International Union (SEIU) and the Hotel Employees and Restaurant Employees Union (HERE) had in recent successful organizing campaigns. The sale of Gargiulo to pro-union investors, for example, was a major accomplishment of the corporate campaign. A savvy and effective use of the media to garner the support of the general public was a second major part of the corporate campaign. Here, too, the UFW was highly successful.

The third component of the drive, the *grassroots campaign,* was carried out in the local community and in the fields. It involved establishing relationships with crew leaders and individual pickers. It was at this level that the UFW was least successful. While the union performed very well in its political and corporate campaigns, it was never able to make significant inroads at the grassroots level. I have described in previous chapters how the organizational structure of Coastal Berry changed after it was sold and explained how this affected the sorts of relationships the UFW was able to establish with company personnel. The union's limited success at this level ultimately cost it a victory in the fields. I begin my analysis with the political campaign because it set the larger context for much that occurred during the unionization drive.

The Political and Legal Campaign

The first aspect of the political campaign to consider is the mediatory role of the Agricultural Labor Relations Board (ALRB). I approach this aspect with a brief background to the tension-filled relationships among the UFW, the grower community, and the labor board. I then discuss the important decisions taken by the board during the campaign and interpret the implications of these decisions for the various interested parties. A second important aspect of the campaign is the relationship between the UFW and political and labor elites. That relationship is noteworthy because political affiliations were instrumental in the sale of the Gargiulo Company. This leads into a discussion of the corporate campaign, the second component of the UFW's organization drive.

The ALRB has always maintained a precarious position in agribusiness labor relations, and this campaign was no exception. The fundamental source of the quandary is rooted in the board's principle function: to balance competing interests and adjudicate among various parties that are usually at odds with one another. In itself this is not necessarily a problematic position. The problem, rather, arises from the fact that the ALRB has never been able to sustain a requisite level of neutrality. From its inception, the agency has been plagued by accusations of favoritism from both organized labor and the grower community. According to Paul Richardson, general counsel of the ALRB, "The problem with the agency from day one is that it has been more of a political football than it should have been. We need to earn credibility on both sides to be effective" (Alvarez 1999).

The board's credibility is challenged because its five members and one general counsel are appointed by the governor of the state. The makeup of the ALRB is therefore susceptible to the influence of political pressure and lobbying, which has been evident since the Agricultural

Labor Relations Act was created in 1975 during the tenure of liberal Democratic governor Jerry Brown. During this early period the UFW enjoyed a close relationship with the ALRB, with growers grumbling about the imbalance of power on the board. Later, during the administrations of Republican governors George Deukmejian and Pete Wilson, the interests of growers were more strongly represented on the board. In 1986, a frustrated Cesar Chavez went so far as to call for the abolishment of the board because it had become such an impediment to labor organizing. The curtailed activities of the UFW during the 1980s and early 1990s meant that the board was not as politicized as it had been, but probably neither side missed the fact that the strawberry campaign was taking place during a period of transition from a Republican- to a Democratic-appointed board.

The Agricultural Labor Relations Act was modeled after the National Labor Relations Act to deal with two parties: an employer and a labor union. In most cases the labor union has been the UFW. Thus, neither the board nor the UFW were prepared for the unusual appearance of the Comité. Its emergence is significant in that for the first time in the history of ALRB-adjudicated labor disputes, the principle litigants were not a union and a grower, but rather two unions, each claiming to be the legitimate representative of worker interests. This put the ALRB in a predicament since its function is ostensibly to arbitrate between the interests of growers and labor. The ALRB was not intended to mediate labor disputes between two potential bargaining agents.

The actions of the ALRB during the first election reveal that it was guided by a predominant concern for workers' rights to representative elections, despite the possibility of controversy arising from such events. According to the board's website, the agency has two principle functions. Its first function is "To determine and implement, through secret ballot elections, the right of agricultural employees to choose whether or not they wish to be represented by a labor organization for the purpose of collective bargaining with their employer." Commitment to this function is likely the reason that the ARLB decided to grant the Comité an election in 1998 despite the strong objections of the UFW. This decision angered the UFW. Clearly upset by the turn of events, UFW president Arturo Rodriguez went so far as to accuse the board of racial misconduct: "I am just beginning to smell racism on the part of the ALRB. It refuses to treat us, a predominantly Mexican union, in a way that other unions are treated" (Brazil 1998). Despite Rodriguez's sense of victimization and injustice, the UFW was clearly the superior legal force in the court battles that dominated the end of the campaign.

The UFW attempted to have the first election nullified with a combination of public pressure from politicians and concerned citizens and a legal offensive challenging the validity of the proceedings. Several demonstrations were held in protest of the election. In Sacramento and Salinas, vigils were held outside the offices of the ALRB, asking that the election be blocked. At the state capitol, several legislators, including Senator Hilda L. Solis, chair of the State Senate Industrial Relations Committee, lobbied the board on behalf of the union, pressing ALRB general counsel Paul Richardson to stop the petition for an election filed by what they claimed to be a sham union that was employer dominated. Richardson responded, saying, "We still have to do what we have to do, which is fairly evaluate the facts. It's real important that no one misconstrues that it is the voice of the farm worker we are trying to hear and whose voice we are trying to protect" (Henshaw 1998). At a joint legislative hearing before the Senate Industrial Relations Committee held on July 28, 1998, the UFW formally objected to the Comité and the election proceedings. Ironically, the procedures that made it nearly impossible for the UFW to block the first election were the same procedures that the UFW fought to include in the original draft of the Agricultural Labor Relations Act to ensure that growers would not be able to impede the expedient administration of a union election.[1]

The UFW's legal offensive against Coastal Berry and the Comité centered on what the union alleged to be a work environment rife with worker intimidation and coercion surrounding the election. It pointed to the July 1 violence against pro-union supporters as evidence of this hostile environment. Later, the union would argue that an outcome-determinative number of workers had been disenfranchised from the company's Southern California operation. In theory, if all the workers left off voter rolls had voted for the UFW, then the UFW, not the Comité, would have been the winner of the election. A problem arose, however, because the ALRB did not know how to deal with the objections against the election filed by the union and its supporters. At issue was whether the union and individual workers were entitled to file objections since they were not parties in the election proceedings. There was no adequate precedent to determine whether the UFW or pro-UFW employees had standing to submit election objections. Although Section 1156.3(c) of the act states that "within five days after an election, *any person* may file with the board a signed petition," objecting to the election, procedurally, "any person" has referred to parties directly involved in the election (emphasis added).[2]

It would take the ALRB three months to decide whether to accept these complaints. In case number 24 ALRB No. 4, the board ruled 3 to 2 against allowing the UFW objections to stand. The lead opinion found that "despite its literal appeal, this Board, like the NLRB, has construed the scope of 'persons' with standing in election proceedings to apply to only those individuals or entities who possess the requisite direct interest in the election" (p. 7). The issue was skirted by the union when David Gladstone, owner of Coastal Berry—and considered a party in the election—filed objections very similar to those presented by the UFW and its supporters. It was these objections that the board considered in deciding to reject the 1998 election.

Emerging from the objections was the question of whether Coastal Berry's northern and southern operations should be treated as one or two bargaining units. The way the matter was addressed typifies the role of political influence in ALRB proceedings. In November 1998, Fred Capuyan, ALRB regional director in Salinas, recommended that Coastal Berry be treated as one bargaining unit. Based on this initial ruling, a hearing officer recommended that the Watsonville election results be invalidated because 162 workers in Ventura County to the south had not been notified of the election. The board was to meet to determine the validity of this ruling. Two days before the meeting was to be held on January 28, it was canceled. The meeting was postponed ostensibly because the board was unable to reach a quorum with only two sitting members present. Three seats on the board were vacant because recently elected Governor Davis had not yet appointed people to these positions. In an unprecedented move, the governor appointed three high-ranking Democrats to the ALRB for a day, long enough for the ALRB to achieve a quorum and vote to further postpone a vote to certify the Coastal Berry election. The postponement of the meeting would ensure that Democratic-appointed board members would hear the case, thus increasing the likelihood of a ruling that would favor the UFW.

After sixteen years of Republican administrations, the UFW was pleased with the one-day appointment of Democrat board members. "We hope this is a sign that this is a new era," said UFW spokesman Marc Grossman (Lifsher 1999). The grower community was less enthusiastic. According to Comité attorney Jim Gumberg, "It's an inappropriate influence by a political body in the administrative process, and politics shouldn't come into play in a decision like this" (Clark 1999). This was a significant blow for the Comité. Had the board ruled that in fact the company should be divided into two bargaining units, then the vote from the southern region would have been invalidated, but the Comité would have been able to become the bargaining agent in Santa Cruz and Salinas counties, which is what it wanted in the first place.[3] A Davis-appointed board later found that the company should be associated with a single bargaining unit, thus invalidating the entire election.

Later that year, in May 1999, the UFW filed a petition for certification seeking an election in a statewide unit. Incorrectly assuming that it could only get on the ballot if it agreed to a statewide bargaining unit, the Comité reluctantly agreed, although its preference was for two distinct units.[4] The Comité did, however, request that the ballots from both areas be kept separate. During the first election neither group received a majority of votes, so a runoff election was held. The final tally of the runoff election votes, split by region, favored the Comité in the north (448 to 295) and the UFW in the south (321 to 277).

Using tactics traditionally used by growers to stall election certification, the UFW filed hundreds of unfair labor practices petitions (ULPs) against the Comité and the company during the second election, in which it was an intervening party. While some of these objections were certainly valid, many were frivolous and based on speculation or hearsay. For example, objection numbers 46 through 53 dealt with conduct that occurred after the election, when a foreman donned a "no UFW" cap, therefore violating company neutrality. Another objection was based on worker testimony regarding a "conspiratorial meeting" on the edge of the field between allegedly pro-Comité workers and supervisors. By flooding the court with ULPs, the UFW forced the ALRB to investigate each objection, thus stalling certification. When the ALRB did not address these objections expediently, the UFW accused it of dragging its feet.

The ALRB found the most credible objection submitted by the UFW to be one concerning the appropriate scope of the bargaining unit. The Comité countered that the board should not consider the objection since the UFW had sought a statewide bargaining unit and the board had agreed to it. On procedural grounds the board sided with the UFW and agreed to review the scope of the unit. In deciding the scope of the bargaining unit, investigative hearing examiner (IHE) Judge Thomas Sobel reviewed the organizational structure of the Coastal Berry Company. He found that while the company exemplified a high degree of administrative centralization, there was little employee interchange between the two areas. Furthermore, he was persuaded by the UFW's contention that much of the day-to-day operations were subject to local control. He noted, "So thoroughly has the UFW mined the Employee Handbook for examples of local discretion that to repeat all it has discovered would unduly burden this decision" (ALRB 1999). The IHE found that while the work and terms of employment were the same, pay rates were slightly higher in Watsonville and Salinas. Furthermore, there was little common supervision between the two areas. Based on these factors, the IHE decided that workers in the two regions did not share a community of interest and should therefore be treated as two separate units. The decision by the IHE to split the bargaining unit favored the UFW's organizational strengths and strained the Comité's already meager resources. As the product of the social networks found in the company's Northern California operations, the Comité did not enjoy the support in the south that it did in the north. Nor were patron-client relations based on family networks the same obstacle in the south as they were in the Pajaro Valley. The company's Southern California operations had not developed the same level of independence and autonomy as in the north. Thus, family networks and patron-client relations were not imbedded in the organizational structure of the company's southern operations in the same way that they were in the Pajaro Valley. This did not stop the Comité from trying to organize in the south, however. Eddie Hernández recalls the difficulties they faced trying to do this,

> Nosotros solamente fuimos tres días, tres días. Salíamos como a estas horas, toda la noche de camino, llegábamos desvelados, sin asearse y no mas nos trataban de locos. Pero con esos tres días ganamos muchísimos puntos. Si nos vieran dado chanza un mes y si alguien nos hubiera apoyado económicamente para comida, para hospedaje, para gasolina, hubiéramos triunfado profundamente allá. Y ellos estaban meses. Tenían casa, tenían carros, los organizadores (We only went three days, three days. We would leave about this time [7:30 p.m. or so], drive all night, arrive exhausted without having cleaned up, and they treated us as if we were crazy. But with those three days we won many points. If we would have had more opportunities [to travel south], and if someone had supported us economically for food, for housing, and gasoline, we would have profoundly succeeded there. And they [the UFW] were there months. Their organizers had housing and transportation.) [July 2000]

These comments highlight the Comité as a localized phenomenon that emerged from a specific set of social relations found only in the company's operations around the Watsonville area. The difficulties they encountered demonstrate that they were not a fully formed organization capable of successfully competing against the UFW.

Ultimately, Eddie Hernández, Jim Gumberg, and the rest of the Comité were vastly overwhelmed by the UFW's robust political and legal resources. The fact that Gumberg, a management-side labor lawyer, was not familiar with the Agricultural Labor Relations Act did not help the Comité. According to the presiding IHE, the confusion surrounding the post-2000 election litigation was caused by the lack of understanding of ALRB procedures by the Comité. The technical details of the legal proceedings also alienated workers who did not have a clear understanding of American jurisprudence. Workers for and against the UFW became tired and frustrated of multiple elections and the lack of final outcome over the course of two years. Regardless, it is difficult to conceive that Gumberg, taking on the case pro bono, would have had the ability to singlehandedly litigate against the UFW's legal team, headed by Marcos Camacho, who was accustomed to dealing exclusively with the labor act and had a much greater understanding of the intricacies of the labor board and its procedures. Perhaps Judge Thomas Sobel put it best when he wrote in his findings, "In other words, the Committee [Comité] thought the election was over because it had won: Board processes are rarely so simple, not just for the Committee, but for all unions and all employers alike" (ALRB 1999: 20).

Not only was the UFW equipped with formidable legal resources, it also maintained an impressive roster of political allies. In fact, several national Democratic politicians played critical roles in the 1997 sale of the Gargiulo Company to two Maryland investors. After Rodriguez took the helm of the union in 1994, he reestablished ties to the AFL-CIO, national and state-level politicians, church groups, and Latino civil rights organizations. The union also expanded its role in California politics, once again becoming a big contributor to the Democratic Party and actively taking positions on ballot initiatives such as campaigning against Proposition 187 in 1996 and against Proposition 227 in 1998.[5] This political activity, and the allegiances created in the process, would be a major contributing factor in the sale of Gargiulo, a transaction that was the cornerstone of the UFW's corporate campaign against the strawberry industry.

The Corporate Campaign

Pioneered in the late 1970s and early 1980s, corporate campaigns originally focused on pressuring the corporate boards of recalcitrant employers (Bronfenbrenner and Juravich 2001). Later efforts evolved to encompass a variety of tactics employed to disrupt an employer's business dealings, affecting relations with investors, lenders, consumers, clients, and subsidiaries. According to Rachel Sherman and Kim Voss, "In corporate campaigns, unions do sophisticated research and financial analysis in order to find ways to attack the employer's image, profits, and ability to conduct business as usual; organizers describe this as 'finding the Achilles' heel' of the company" (2000: 85). An example of this can be found in the Justice for Janitors campaign in Los Angeles during the late 1980s. The union hired a full-time researcher to study the cleaning firms operating in the city's downtown buildings. Based on information gathered, workers initiated media-oriented events that targeted specific individuals or companies hiring non-union cleaning firms, not only causing embarrassment but also raising public awareness of the plight of workers (Milkman and Wong 2000).

The UFW employed a similarly broad array of tactics during the strawberry campaign. As in past organizing efforts, the union incorporated a variety of strategies that extended beyond the boundaries of the worksite in its efforts to mobilize workers. The rest of this section analyses two broad elements of the corporate campaign: the UFW's public relations strategies and the union's successful efforts to transfer ownership of the Gargiulo Company to union-friendly investors.

The UFW launched a public-information campaign on November 13, 1996, at the AFL-CIO headquarters in Washington D.C., where the previous month, newly elected AFL-CIO president John Sweeney had declared the strawberry campaign the most important unionization drive in the country and had pledged the full support of the AFL-CIO to the effort. At a press conference and rally that featured speakers from the National Organization of Women (NOW) and the National Association for the Advancement of Colored People (NAACP), UFW president Arturo Rodriguez outlined the two major goals of the public awareness campaign. First, the campaign would inform the public about the deplorable working conditions in the strawberry fields. Second, it would get supermarket managers to sign a pledge demanding that strawberry producers sign an industry-wide labor agreement with the union. While falling just short of an actual boycott, the grower industry felt the campaign held the implied threat of a boycott should the demand for an industry-wide contract not be met. The campaign was accompanied by the release of the "Five Cents for Fairness" report.

The "Five Cents for Fairness" report was followed by numerous press releases from the UFW media relations office chronicling the campaign. These statements were valuable forms of communication with the general public—particularly in 1997 and 1998, when the UFW uncovered the financial association between several industry groups and some of the anti-UFW workers' organizations that had emerged in the area. The union effectively projected its findings onto the general public with the generation of informative news accounts that consistently made their way into local and national media outlets. A press packet released during this time included newspaper accounts with relevant background information and copies of checks from industry groups to anti-UFW worker organizations.

The grower community and workers were not nearly as effective as the UFW in expressing their positions to a wide audience. Grower perspectives on the campaign were usually published in limited-release newsletters or industry publications such as *Ag Alert*, the weekly newspaper of the California Farm Bureau Federation, or the Western Growers Association Newsletter. Mark Munger, marketing director of Driscoll Associates, remembers being blindsided by the media activity surrounding the campaign. In an October 2000 interview, Munger complained about being distracted by UFW press releases and recalled being unable to counter the claims of the union in the local press. This inability to communicate effectively with the general public was especially troublesome when members of the industry were clearly implicated in supporting local anti-UFW groups. The UFW was able to launch a well-coordinated offensive of legal action coupled with widely released press reports against which the industry was largely helpless.

Similarly, the various anti-UFW groups that emerged, including the Comité, were unable to convey their message to the general public because they lacked the skills, knowledge, and organizational infrastructure of an effective media relations department. This demonstrates a lack of organizational capacity found in formally structured groups. For example, Comité lawyer Jim Gumberg recalls his difficulty reaching reporters who were basing stories on UFW press reports. He also recalled frustration with having his responses to local editorials declined by editors. Comité leader Eddie Hernández experienced similar dismissals by local Spanish-speaking news outlets. The UFW's effective use of the news media allowed it to shape popular opinion about the campaign to a large degree. Neither the growers nor the workers groups came close to affecting popular opinion in the way the UFW did.

Evidence of both groups' lack of effectiveness in shaping public opinion can be found in a 1998 visit by St. Louis clergy members to the Central Coast, arranged by the UFW and paid for by the Driscoll cooperative. In June 1998, three Catholic clergy—Friar Steve Joyce, Friar Steve Robeson, and Alicia Alvarado—visited fields owned by four Driscoll growers in the Central Coast region. The visit had been suggested by Schnuck, a large Midwestern supermarket chain that sold Driscoll strawberries. In an interview, Mark Munger stated that Driscoll had originally conceived of the visit as a good way for a neutral third party to assess conditions in local fields. During their visit, the clergy members spoke with pickers in the fields and in their homes, and discussed the organizing drive with Driscoll officials.

The findings of the Catholic group's report were mixed. The clergy members found clean toilets but also a "frantic" work pace and were concerned about allegations of working "off the clock" and working long hours without a break. Most interesting about the visit is that while it was initially welcomed and paid for by Driscoll, it was the UFW who took the credit for and benefited from the visit. Munger complained about "continuously being left out of the darn thing," particularly after the clergy returned to St. Louis (October 2000). The visit was widely publicized, with Driscoll shown in a negative light. Perhaps most frustrating to Munger was that the cooperative was being vilified in the press even though the union was not attempting to organize any Driscoll growers.

The UFW was not only savvy in its relationship to local and national media; it was equally astute in its dealings with prominent political and labor groups. Such relationships would serve it well in the sale of the Gargiulo Company to union-friendly investors. Without the help of influential labor leaders and prominent Democrats, the UFW would have been unable to orchestrate the sale of Gargiulo. This assistance from powerful players is important to keep in mind because Coastal Berry did not become the focus of the UFW campaign because of work-related conditions. It became the focus because, for several reasons that will be explained in greater detail below, the company presented the UFW and the AFL-CIO with an ideal setting from which to organize the whole industry. If the UFW and the AFL-CIO could organize the largest producer in the region, they would have a solid basis from which to organize the entire industry. In this sense, Coastal Berry was the "Achilles' heel" of the Central Coast strawberry industry.

The Gargiulo sale links the political and corporate strategies of the UFW strawberry campaign. Without political allies or the resources and networks of the AFL-CIO, the sale of the company may not have occurred. The Gargiulo Company was one division of a small subsidiary owned by the Monsanto Corporation, one of the largest agro-industrial chemicals firms in the world. The Central Coast strawberry operation was not Gargiulo's primary focus; the company was mainly involved in growing tomatoes. As an industry leader in genetic modification, Monsanto had purchased Gargiulo to research the feasibility of genetically engineered tomatoes. The acquisition of Gargiulo's strawberry division on the Central Coast provided the opportunity to expand into other genetically engineered crops. At the time, Gargiulo was the only non-locally owned strawberry company in the region.

Intent on maintaining a positive relationship with the general public, Monsanto was not keen on receiving the negative publicity that an extended unionization campaign might bring.[6] "We're a public company that is very sensitive to its image," stated company spokesman Philip Angell (Lifsher 1998). At the same time, according to Monsanto, the company was consolidating its holdings to concentrate exclusively on biotechnology and genetics. In early May 2000, officials from Monsanto, the UFW, and the AFL-CIO met in Washington, D.C., to discuss the terms of a potential sale. Then Vice President Al Gore, Missouri Congressman Richard Gephardt, and Mickey Kantor, Monsanto director and former commerce secretary under President Clinton, were also involved in the negotiations. The sale of Gargiulo was a good business decision for Monsanto for several reasons. In the larger context of Monsanto's extensive holdings, the strawberry division of Gargiulo was almost insignificant. According to the California Farm Bureau Federation, strawberries accounted for less than 1 percent of Monsanto's annual gross income (Sotero 2000). The loss of profits would be a small price to pay to avoid unwanted negative publicity. It also would allow Monsanto the opportunity to sell assets not directly related to its new focus.

The Coastal Berry Company's new owners, David Gladstone and Landon Butler, were financiers from Maryland who invested union pension funds.[7] The two had close ties to organized labor, but they had no holdings or prior experience in agribusiness. They promptly signed a neutrality agreement with the UFW and renamed the company Coastal Berry. Six months later, in December 1997, Butler would sell his interest in the firm to Gladstone.

Almost immediately, the grower community responded very negatively to the sale. A consortium of grower groups filed unfair labor practices against the UFW, Monsanto, and Gargiulo, claiming the sale of the company was unlawful. The lawsuits pointed to a June 17, 1997, press release from Monsanto and the AFL-CIO that stated, "The agreement is intended to result in the scheduling of a supervised election consistent with the California Labor Relations Act as soon as practical, with the details and timing to be worked out by representatives [of the company] and union representatives." Growers also felt affronted by Monsanto. According to David Moore, president of the Western Growers Association (WGA), "We cannot understand why [Monsanto chairman Robert] Shapiro has failed to communicate with California Agriculture, one of Monsanto's biggest customers. I have to ask, is it because he knows the potential harm he has caused our industry and is too embarrassed to talk to us about it?" (Western Growers Association

Newsletter, 23 June 1997). Shortly thereafter, UFW vice president Dolores Huerta dismissed the charges. "It is sad that the WGA is trying to stand in the way of this hopeful breakthrough," she said at a Sacramento press conference. "The unfair labor charges are ridiculous" (Sotero 1997).

The sale allowed the UFW a degree of influence over the company. According to organizer Katie Manning, "There was a lot of pressure from the AFL-CIO because those people invest lots of union pension funds, those two guys, so there was always the threat with them, if you don't do the right thing with the UFW, then we're going, the AFL-CIO would say, we're going to tell our member unions to pull their pension funds from you [the investors], which is like millions of dollars" (August 2000). The close rapport between the UFW and Coastal Berry did not last long, however. The relationship soured in the aftermath of the events surrounding the July 1998 work stoppages and demonstrations instigated by anti-UFW forces. Shortly after these events the UFW began to privately demand that Coastal Berry dismiss several ringleaders of the anti-UFW movement; publicly, the UFW accused the company of condoning anti-UFW activity. According to ALRB records,

> Respondent [Coastal Berry] continued to receive reports of employee dissatisfaction, and conflicts between pro- and anti-UFW workers. At the same time, it was subjected to repeated accusations of anti-UFW conduct by UFW representatives, in particular, its president, Arturo Rodriguez. The UFW demanded that supervisors and employees perceived as opposed to it be discharged for violating a neutrality agreement adopted by Respondent from its predecessor, and/or for coercing pro-UFW employees, and that pro-UFW employees discharged when Galper was president be rehired. (ALRB 1999b: 6)

For his part Gladstone felt offended and victimized by what he perceived to be the UFW's uncomfortably close relationship to Coastal Berry and resented being told how to run the company (ibid). According to the same document, the UFW presented Coastal Berry with a list of twenty employees it wanted to have dismissed. In January 1998 and February 1999, eleven of the workers on the UFW list were discharged. The workers filed charges against what they claimed to be unlawful termination of employment. In December 1999, an administrative law judge found that the workers had engaged in a protected law stoppage and that by dismissing them from work after signing a document stating that no such action would be taken, company president David Smith had violated section 1153(a) of the labor act. The court also found Smith to be a generally unreliable witness with a tendency to exaggerate the threat to person and property during the various demonstrations and stoppages. Shortly after the last worker was discharged in February 1999, Smith resigned as president of the company. As Coastal Berry's first president after the sale, Smith presided over an unintended course of events. The changes made at Coastal Berry after it was purchased in the summer of 1997 reveal how these events took place.

The Grassroots Campaign

The grassroots campaign includes the micro-level exchanges that occurred on a day-to-day basis among the members of the various interested parties. These exchanges were manifest as encounters between the UFW and Coastal Berry personnel, including the Comité and its supporters. To understand these face-to-face interactions, it is necessary to consider the organizational context that structured such exchanges. It is important to recall that even though the social milieu in which the campaign occurred included the physical spaces of the worksite and people's homes, these exchanges were governed by a set of social relations based on workplace hierarchy and status relations. To understand how these power dynamics affected the outcome of the campaign, it is necessary to understand authority relations within the organizational structure at Coastal Berry.

Coastal Berry's outsider ownership, vertically integrated production structure, and unusually large size all had a significant impact on the nature and course of the UFW campaign. The same characteristics also made it susceptible to a union organizing campaign. As I will explain, however, these are the very reasons that the union had such a difficult time organizing the company's workers. In what follows I expand on the social relations among the various strata at the company and examine the organization of production before and after the company was sold. At the close of this section, I examine how mid-level managers affected the outcome of the campaign.

Chapter 4 outlined the dominant features of the Central Coast strawberry industry. The industry had many small producers with strong local ties. The small size of most operations engendered a degree of reciprocity and exchange between workers and owners that is unusual in California's commercial agriculture. Coastal Berry farmed 1,250 acres in the Central Coast region. Its large size meant that it did not comprise social relations of production similar to those of other strawberry producers. In this respect Coastal Berry was an anomaly. The fact that the company was not locally owned was also out of the norm in the strawberry industry. While large corporate concerns dominate fruit and vegetable production in California, the strawberry industry is still the domain of small local farmers. The company was also unique among Central Coast strawberry producers in that it handled its own cooling and shipping. As stated in Chapter 4, most growers in the region are affiliated with one of various cooler-shipper cooperatives.

Because it is neither locally owned nor a member of a cooperative, Coastal Berry lacked the ties of solidarity that have emerged among local strawberry producers through historical, familial, and economic relations. As a result, the company was not generally perceived by local producers as having the same stake in the well-being of the region and the industry. This isolation was further exacerbated by the fact that the company maintained its own cooling and shipping facilities. Because Coastal Berry managed its entire production and distribution process, its foremen and supervisors did not have daily contact with other growers in the area who are part of the local cooperatives or other cooler-shipper associations. Most strawberry farmers make daily trips to the cooler cooperatives with which they are affiliated and attend regularly scheduled member meetings. This sort of frequent, face-to-face interaction among a familiar and trusted group of growers was essential during the early phases of the UFW campaign, when the grower community began to circle the proverbial wagons and strategize over what to do regarding the impending unionization efforts. The limited interaction between Coastal Berry managers and others in the industry created some distance between it and the rest of the grower community throughout much of the campaign. To a large degree the company found itself "out of the loop" of local farmers. Its insularity, large size, and outside ownership made the company a target for the UFW.[8]

The sale of Gargiulo was disruptive to its organizational structure. Even though the basic configuration of the organization remained the same, interactions between the various strata of workers changed drastically between 1998 and 2000. These changes were a consequence of actions taken by the UFW to place the company in a more favorable position for achieving the union's goals.

Before and after the sale of Gargiulo, the company had four general categories of personnel.[9] The uppermost stratum consisted of the president and the professional support staff, including soil and pest scientists, the sales and marketing team, and the general administrative team. This group had responsibility for the overall productivity and efficiency of the enterprise. Employees in this category did not manage the actual planting and harvesting of strawberries, and they thus had limited contact with workers in the fields. The second personnel category comprised mid-level managers and supervisors. These employees served as intermediaries between the crews in the field and the dictates of the president and professional staff; often, they were workers who had risen through the ranks of the company. It was their job to ensure that production quotas were met and to oversee the planting, maintenance, and harvesting of the fruit.

The third category of personnel at Gargiulo consisted of better-paid farmworkers, including foremen/women who served as crew chiefs in addition to truck and tractor drivers, crate loaders, card punchers, and irrigators. Some of these positions require special skills or technical expertise, such as the ability to drive a tractor or knowledge of irrigation systems. Others, such as card puncher or crate loader, require no such specialization. The jobs in this category that require special skills or knowledge tend to command wages that are better than those of the average picker.[10] Unskilled, better-paid employees earned slightly more than pickers, the fourth category. Regardless of the relatively small pay difference between workers in this category and pickers, these positions are highly coveted because of their relative ease. For some jobs, such as tractor driver and irrigation worker, employment can extend past the harvesting season, which also makes these jobs more attractive. Pickers comprise the largest category of personnel in the organization. Coastal Berry president Earnie Farley told me, "Without them the whole operation breaks down." It is to these individuals that the UFW devoted its grassroots organizing efforts.

Although there was some dissatisfaction within the organization prior to the 1997 sale of the company, the majority of workers I interviewed seemed content with their experiences at Gargiulo during Larry Galper's tenure as general manager. Subsequent conversations with others at different positions within the company's organizational structure led me to believe that the workers' favorable views of the company were a result of good leadership. Galper fostered a high degree of interaction among the different strata of the company, which not only facilitated formation of an efficient production team but also helped minimize discontent. While acknowledging the problems with the company, anti-UFW leader Eddie Hernández maintained it was a good place to work: "There was favoritism, but the people were at peace and accepted this because the work and the work conditions were good. We had water, toilets, the foremen wouldn't rush us, rather we worked at pace, there wasn't so much pressure." This contentment among workers, enabled and reinforced by the company's coherent organizational structure, ended with the sale of Gargiulo to Landon Butler and David Gladstone in 1997.

As was noted in an earlier chapter, Gargiulo had always been divided into two divisions, inland and coastal. It was with the various ranches of the coastal division that the UFW was able to make the greatest inroads with individual workers. The inland division was run by a clique of family and friends related to a supervisor named Enrique Leal.[11] This group maintained fairly strong control over the workforce in that area. The power of the Leal group in the coastal division presented few problems during Galper's tenure because the strong vertical integration present in the company helped to mitigate the overextension of power. The dismissal of Galper and other high-level employees would alter the balance of power within the company hierarchy.

After the sale, mid-level foremen and supervisors gained significant power over the lives of Coastal Berry's pickers. Coastal Berry became a decentralized work environment where control over work conditions was exclusively held by these supervisors and foremen, at least as far as the workers were concerned. While workers may not have known who the company's president was, they knew that Enrique Leal was the head supervisor at Coastal. They also knew that Leal had placed many people in positions of power at the company. Enrique Leal and his network had the power to hire, fire, or promote workers or make workers' experiences easy or difficult on the job. Their positions of power had furthermore earned them a cadre of loyal followers among the loaders, punchers, truck drivers, and other individuals who had obtained their choice positions through these managers. One UFW organizer had a clear sense that this aggregation of power was happening. When asked why the UFW had failed to penetrate the company's inland division she said, "In Riverside [an inland ranch] the supervisor and then assistant supervisor had a lot of people from their town in Mexico come over and work for them. They also had houses in Watsonville that they rented out to workers. They paid the coyote for a lot of workers. So there was a lot of modern-day transnational indebted servitude, you know. That, and they were never able to correctly identify the leadership there" (interview 2000).[12]

As is often the case with newly acquired power that is not democratically sanctioned, this recently empowered group became despotic. Nepotism increased, along with the incidence of random and arbitrary uses and abuses of power. There was no systematic or rule-based system for decision making, and judgments were subject to the whims of people in power at the time. These conditions made for a volatile and uncertain work environment. During the period following the sale of Gargiulo, worker dissatisfaction increased. One union supporter said,

En el trabajo lo discriminan a uno así de, no hay señoría ni este, para promociones de trabajo así nada. Mas discriminan a cierta forma de que por ser amigo del mayordomo le dan el mejor trabajo a aquel y uno por que no tiene amistades lo van dejando abajo. Y así ha estado siempre. (At work they discriminate against one in that there is no seniority, nor job promotions nor anything. The discrimination takes a certain form whereby being friends with the foreman, they give that person a better job, and one who doesn't have friends is being left behind. And that's the way it's always been.) [September 2000]

Another woman spoke of her friend who had been working for eighteen seasons hoping to be offered a puncher's position only to see that job go to a younger woman who had been working two years. It is no surprise that that the UFW found willing ears for its message of a hiring hall, a formal grievance procedure, and the end to arbitrary power among the foremen and supervisors. When the UFW orchestrated the sale of the company, it unwittingly triggered a chain of events that in many ways would undermine its organizing efforts. The change in the top leadership of the company and concomitant decrease in vertical integration led to the consolidation of power among the Leal network, in which favoritism and arbitrary use of power was rampant. The latter led to greater worker discontent and amenability to collective action, but not necessarily UFW support.

Such worker insecurity and dissatisfaction created an opening for the Comité, which gained widespread support among workers. It is not accurate to simply say that the Comité was controlled by foremen and supervisors, or that it was a company union. Its emergence is rooted in several important concerns among company personnel. The early Comité consisted of workers frustrated by poor and persistent organizing by the UFW. It was supported by supervisors and foremen because a UFW victory would have curbed its power and influence in the company. But it is not accurate to say that the Comité was completely controlled by these power brokers. As the idea of the Comité gained momentum, it gradually began to assert its independence from the core managerial power at the company. Key figures in the movement, such as Eddie Hernández and Francisco Lobato, saw the Comité as a viable, independent vehicle with which to curb the excesses of the UFW and of mid-level managers. This idea resonated with many workers who had to cope with the unwanted advances of the UFW along with the arbitrary uses of power by the managers in charge of their daily lives.

The Comité was unable to deliver on its promises, however. Having come to power on a platform based on ousting the UFW, it was ill-equipped to operate as a labor union. It was, however, able to secure higher wages for pickers than the UFW ($6.50 versus $6.25, according to their respective contracts). Still, it lacked the skills necessary to effectively go about the day-to-day business of a union. Aware of the promises of unionization, workers expected the Comité to deliver. When it did not, pickers became disillusioned. According to one worker,

> O sea la gente que no, que no apoyaba a la unión, ya esta mirando ahorita el cambio que los del comité no han hecho nada, ni va a ser nada. Y ya ahorita están muchos cambiando de parecer. donde esta lo que les prometió. (The people that didn't support the [UFW] are now seeing the change, that the Comité hasn't done anything, nor is it going to do anything. And right now many are changing their way of thinking. Where is what they promised?) [September 2000]

Two years later, in 2002, workers voted to make the UFW their bargaining agent.

The Paradox of Farm Labor Organizing

The history of labor organization at Coastal Berry illustrates the paradox of farm labor organizing. The case of Coastal Berry suggests that growers most likely to be targeted for unionization campaigns are not those who employ workers most in need of unionization. Employers most vulnerable to the types of tactics employed by the UFW, such as major public campaigns designed to put pressure on recognizable products, are most able to treat their workers well because they have the resources to do so. As grower attorney James Sullivan stated at the beginning of the campaign, "The industry is very fragmented and very diverse, and labor conditions are all over the map. Some growers offer terrific wages with full benefits, and some are backwards" (Lordan 1996). In a highly competitive market that is driven to high standards of quality, farmers who can afford to pay for top-quality work will do so because they know that quality products command the highest prices on the market. These farmers are the ones who not only pay better wages but also provide workers with benefits including health care. Because workers on these farms command higher wages and receive greater benefits, they are not as likely to feel ill will toward their employers.

Small producers, operating at the margins of the industry and struggling to make ends meet, are the most likely to engage in disingenuous practices. Because of their small scale and precarious finances, however, these growers are least likely to withstand a union's sustained organizing campaign. This condition is bad for a union because if workers lose jobs due to an organizing campaign, the union's reputation is tarnished; people begin to see the union as an organization that closes farms. In the Central Coast strawberry industry the majority of farmers operating at this level are former pickers themselves; it is difficult for a union to target these former Mexican farmworkers. Small growers have one final defense against unionization: it simply is not cost effective for a union to put time and resources into organizing only twenty or thirty workers.

The unique character of farm labor organizing can be illustrated in a conversation with a local political leader in Watsonville. Tony Campos, the son of a strawberry sharecropper, has had many elected positions in the local community. He recalled a conversation with Irv Hirshenbaum, a UFW vice president,

> He came in there for twenty minutes; we were in there for four, three hours. And I told him, you know, we have a farmer who has his people living in caves, that works his people and once he owes them a lot of money or a good portion of money he calls the migra [immigration services] on them, why don't we go after him? Why don't we make an example of him? Why don't we go in and change his practices. Well, they didn't want to listen about that. I said you wanna concentrate on the big banana but you're letting the little banana slide by, and that's the one who's poisoning the whole thing.

> ... I actually feel a lot of these farmers, I'm not saying all of them, a lot of the major farmers do treat their workers pretty decent. Is it that maybe these guys are being treated pretty damn decent and they don't want to take a chance on something better? That could be it too. I don't think there's anyone out there who wouldn't want to better themselves. But is the risk so big that it's not worth taking? I can't answer that. The only ones that can answer that are the workers. (May 2000)

Coastal Berry was targeted for a unionization campaign for several reasons. Working conditions at the company were not primary among them. Rather, the company had several qualities that made unionization more practical: its large size and outside ownership made it a prime candidate for a protracted political and corporate campaign. One would expect that a poor working environment is a necessary precondition for labor organization, but this case suggests that other factors are more salient.

A lack of poor working conditions at Coastal Berry is only one reason that the UFW encountered difficulties in organizing its workers. Although the UFW was remarkably effective in the political and corporate aspects of the campaign, it failed to win an organizing vote because it was unable to understand the situation at the grassroots level. One may fairly say that the UFW, with the AFL-CIO, won the political and corporate battles but lost the campaign on the ground. The UFW and other unions would do well to recall that organizing campaigns ultimately depend on the rank and file. Economic and political processes facilitate—but do not replace—effective union organizing.

A nuanced analysis of the campaign reveals that the UFW both succeeded and failed. Where it succeeded, it did so because of its superior organizational capacity and its ability to wield institutional leverage among regional and national power brokers. Where it failed, it did so because of its inadequate efforts on the ground. The UFW may also have been a victim of its own success. The same complex bureaucratic structure that enabled it to pursue such sophisticated political and corporate campaigns failed the union when it came to the grassroots. It was because of its rigid top-down approach to the campaign that the union failed to quickly respond to changing conditions in the fields around Watsonville.

The rise and eventual collapse of the Comité also teaches us about immigrant networks and labor unions. These networks consist of incredibly strong bonds among individual workers—bonds that the UFW was never able to break. When the UFW did finally win a contract at Coastal Berry, it did so because of its superior organizational capacity, not because of its ability to win the hearts and minds of workers at the company. The final irony is that the UFW was founded on the strength of interpersonal bonds among farmworkers that were not very different from the interpersonal bonds at Coastal Berry.

---

[1] Section 1156 of the ALRA establishes rules of conduct for representative elections. To request an election, a bargaining agent must submit authorization cards from a majority of the currently employed workforce when employment levels are at least 50 percent of peak. For an election to occur, no valid election may have taken place within the past twelve months, nor can there be a union currently representing workers. Section 1156.3 of the act states that an election must be held within seven days from the date a valid petition for unionization is submitted to the ALRB (if a strike is in progress an election will take place within forty-eight hours). Any disputes arising from the petition are resolved after the election. This procedure ensures that elections are not delayed so that the workforce drops to below 50 percent of peak employment, at which time an election cannot take place.

[2] In the provisions dealing with election procedures the act refers only to "parties." Section 1156.3(c) is the only place where the term "person" appears.

[3] According to Gumberg, the Comité was never interested in the southern region and would have been content as the bargaining agent in the north. At this point the UFW was interested in a single bargaining unit.

[4] According to ALRB transcripts it would have been possible for the Comité to ask for an election against the UFW in the northern region only. See Case No. 99-RC-4-SAL.

[5] Proposition 187 was meant to restrict social services to illegal immigrants. Proposition 227 was supposed to end bilingual education in state schools. Both pieces of legislation were passed by California voters. Proposition 187 was later found unconstitutional by a federal court.

[6] During the Vietnam war, Monsanto has heavily criticized as the manufacturer of the defoliant Agent Orange. More recently, it has been attacked for its promotion and sale of genetically engineered crops.

[7] The fact that they were union investors may be the source of a rumor in the grower community that the company was actually purchased using union pension money.

[8] It is not my intent to oversimplify the relationship between Coastal Berry and other strawberry producers in the Central Coast region. It should be noted, for example, that except for a brief period after it was sold, the president and upper management, as well as foremen and supervisors, have all been locals. This allowed Coastal Berry a certain degree of acceptance among the local farmers. Those I talked to acknowledged knowing some of the managers and president, if not the owners. Most farmers I talked to were quick to point out its anomalous situation as well, however.

[9] This heuristic schema is an approximation of the entire arrangement of workers at the company. Some positions were integral to the overall operation of the company (cooler staff, mechanics, latrine attendants) but are not mentioned here. I omit them from further discussion because of their marginal roles with respect to the campaign.

[10] While the wages of these skilled workers tend to be higher than those of pickers, that is not always true. The wages of pickers are not constant, nor are those of hourly paid tractor drivers or irrigation workers. During the height of the season, when the pay schedule is based on a combination hourly and piece rate, with good weather and plentiful fruit, a picker can see his or her wages rise dramatically.

[11] It was in fact Leal's brother, Sergio, who emerged as a leader of the Comité.

[12] A coyote is a human smuggler.

7

Contexts for Success and Failure

Loosely affiliated individuals can achieve lasting structural change only when they have adopted the organizational template necessary to press social claims via institutional mechanisms. They must operate as formal organizations and apply institutional leverage within a community of neutral, allied, and competing organizations. As we have seen, this was an approach at which the UFW was particularly adept, especially when it came to dealing with the ALRB. The Comité, in contrast, did not know the rules of the game and was therefore unable to compete with the UFW and other groups in its organizational orbit. Its inability to compete is understandable when one considers how social position usually influences what is learned. Like individuals, organizations go through a process of socialization whereby they learn customs and norms of acceptable behavior in their organizational milieu. This process is a significant challenge for organizations comprising individuals such as farmworkers from marginalized backgrounds. Historically, these individuals have not been socially positioned to learn formal rules of organizational exchange, and their collective efforts to bring about social change have been stymied as a result. As this chapter demonstrates, however, these rules are critical if an organization is to have a lasting impact. My own encounter as a researcher with the ALRB's regional director in Salinas helps illustrate why it is important to know the rules of the game.

In the first week of September 2000, I met with Fred Capuyan, the ALRB's regional director of the Salinas office, to try to learn more about the role of the ALRB in the strawberry campaign. Capuyan, a lawyer, was charged with conducting agricultural labor elections in the Central Coast region. The two elections at the Coastal Berry Company had made the past two growing seasons particularly busy for Capuyan and his office, so I was eager to interview him. Unfortunately, I was twenty minutes late because I had had trouble finding the ALRB office in Salinas. When I finally did find the correct office, I rushed in only to be told by a receptionist to wait. Through an open door I could see Capuyan on the phone; he was wearing a suit, so I was glad that I had opted to wear a jacket and tie to the interview—the only time during the research process that I donned such attire. This anecdote is not gratuitous. My instinctive knowledge to wear a suit and tie is a form of cultural capital, which signals an awareness of proper modes of conduct and facilitates exchange within a given social context. Knowledge of institutions and the ability to implement this knowledge is the organizational analogue to cultural capital. However, although I knew what would constitute proper attire in this setting to be taken seriously as a scholar, I was unfamiliar with the details of California agricultural labor law.

For most of the interview, Mr. Capuyan explained the intricacies of the ALRA and procedural dynamics of farm labor unionization in California. Unlike workers in most US states, California farmworkers have the right to organize under the California Agricultural Labor Relations Act of 1975. Capuyan explained that the ALRB, or Ley Laboral, as it was known among workers, administers the act. Its work lies in two main areas. First, the ALRB conducts representative elections and certifies election results. Second, it investigates unfair labor practice (ULP) claims. The ALRB usually delegates responsibility for this task to administrative law judges (ALJs). According to the ALRB website, these judges "take evidence and make initial recommendations in the form of written decisions with respect to issues of fact or law raised by the parties." Parties wishing to challenge the findings of an ALJ may appeal to the ALRB, which then issues its own ruling. Such a ruling can be further challenged in a court of appeals. Capuyan explained how these procedures had worked over the previous two years at Coastal Berry, where two elections had taken place, hundreds of ULPs had been filed, and a single decision from an ALJ had altered the course of unionization in the California strawberry industry. Following, I present a theoretical introduction to organizational fields and institutions and explain how they help to better understand the interorganizational dynamics found in farm labor mobilization.

The ALRB, or Ley Laboral, featured prominently in many of my conversations with Coastal Berry farmworkers, many of whom were resentful toward and angry with the agency regardless of whether they were in favor of the Comité or the UFW. This frustration was well founded: the agency's functioning had never clearly been explained to them. It is ironic that among the many parties involved in the strawberry campaign, farmworkers, whose livelihoods are most directly impacted by the decisions of the ALRB, were the least knowledgeable about the agency. Their ignorance of these affairs arose from the fact that their representative, the Comité, lacked the organizational capacity to compile the institutional knowledge necessary to effectively achieve its objectives in a highly competitive organizational field comprising collective actors with far greater understanding of relevant institutions such as the ALRB. This problem has plagued farmworkers throughout the twentieth century in their attempts to organize.

Playing the Game

Farmworkers have had a difficult time mobilizing because they have not usually been effective actors within their respective organizational fields. An organizational field is any set of organizations that regularly interact with one another. Institutions, as a reminder, may be thought of as the rules that govern conduct within a given organizational fields. A group's organizational capacity enables it to develop the institutional knowledge necessary to successfully compete within a constellation of competing groups: an organizational field. Organizational fields and institutions can help us understand the UFW unionization campaign and other instances of farm labor mobilization. However, I must first elaborate on the concepts before they can be applied to explain what happened at Coastal Berry and other related cases. To meet their objectives, all collective actors, regardless of the organizational field in which they operate, must first become formal organizations and learn "the rules of the game." As sets of rules that govern interactions among all types of organizations, institutions matter immensely. Thus, the concepts of organizational fields and institutions are necessary to understand the outcome of the strawberry unionization campaign in the form of legal rulings.

I will use this theoretical scaffolding to frame the history of interorganizational struggles among farm labor advocates and other collective actors, which led to the creation of an institutional context for labor mobilization. I argue that the Agricultural Labor Relations Act (ALRA) represents the institutionalization of a policy regime to adjudicate labor conflicts in California. By examining the history of labor conflicts, as well as the emergence of successful advocacy organizations among the disenfranchised, we can observe the ways in which collective actors attempt to meet their objectives by operating in organizational fields where they must contend with the actions of like-minded and competing organizations vying for state favor. My historical analysis demonstrates that regardless of the organizational arena, disenfranchised groups have had to learn the rules of the game before they could compete effectively against other organized interests and achieve their goals.

Organizational Fields

Social movement groups such as the Comité and the UFW operate within multi-organizational fields as they attempt to effect social change. These fields represent an organizational environment comprising allied, opposing, and neutral organizations from civil society, the market, and the state, with which social movement groups interact. The concept of organizational fields, introduced in Chapter 2, provides a lens into this organizational context. Various scholars have employed this concept to describe organizations and their interactions (Bourdieu 1977; DiMaggio and Powell 1983; Fligstein 2002; Scott 2004, 2008). Combining existing work on organizational fields, Richard Scott (2008) defines them by the following attributes:

- A diverse array of organizations working within a given arena or domain
- Attention not only to producer organizations but also to their exchange partners, customers, competitors, intermediary actors, regulators, and funding agents
- Recognition that organizations are particularly attentive to and influenced by the existence of other organizations exhibiting the same general features and competing for the same resources

Scott's formulation draws attention to the fact that organizational behavior is embedded within a particular set of interdependent organizations.

The organizational field concept applies to a wide range of organizational groupings. Farm labor advocacy groups, for example, may be located in a field that includes a variety of social movement organizations, funding agencies, community groups, and opposing parties. Other examples of organizational fields are higher education, health care, or a particular industry, such as mobile telephones. The interests of organizations within a field may be complementary or divergent or both. For example, Coke and Pepsi are competitors, but they also share similar interests in that both benefit from an increase in soft drink sales. The same may be said of an agricultural firm and a labor union. While it is in the interests of both that the organization remain profitable and continue with its current levels of employment, there may be disagreement over the conditions of that employment, for example employee benefits. Thus, while some interests may overlap, it is possible that others are at odds.

In the current study the term *agricultural field* is preferable to the term *agriculture industry* because the former incorporates and accounts for both competing and complementary interests. "Industry" reflects merely an orientation toward production and profit. "Field" encapsulates all of the various types of organizations involved in agriculture, including state and advocacy organizations whose objectives are not primarily economic. "Agricultural field" is especially useful when considering the historical development of farm labor mobilization, in which myriad organizations worked both together and in competition to meet their objectives.

The organizational theorist Neil Fligstein (2002) has described markets as a particular type of organizational field. Fligstein posits firm survival rather than profit maximization as the ultimate organizational imperative of for-profit firms operating in markets. In the long term, he asserts, firms benefit more from structured rather than unstructured exchange. He writes, "The seller's organizational survival does not depend on haphazard exchange. It is when the agents in exchange begin to view their own stability (i.e., reproduction) as contingent on stabilizing trade that they turn to socio-organizational vehicles" (2002: 30). It is possible to apply this survival imperative beyond for-profit firms to understand the activities of any organization in any field. To survive, firms and other collective actors rely on their organizational capacity to influence the behavior of other organizational actors. Weberian social power becomes visible in this manner: one entity operating at the interorganizational level influences another even when faced with resistance from that other entity. The Comité's inability to sustain its activities and influence other organizations in its orbit exhibits its lack of social power at the interorganizational level.

Institutions

Organizations create formal and informal rules that govern their interactions. These rules, called *institutions,* influence organizational behavior even as they (the rules) are subject to change by organizations. The ALRA may be considered an institution with formal and informal dimensions. The act is a formal statute enacted into law by the state of the California and designed to regulate farm labor relations. The ALRA also has an administrative apparatus consisting of five board members, administrative law judges, and other employees: it has organizational features. But the ALRA also establishes formal and informal rules of conduct that influence the behavior of other organizations such as labor unions and agricultural employers. The activities of these and other organizations in turn influence the ALRB. For example, because the board's five members and the general counsel are political appointees, they are subject to lobbying by grower and labor interests, which has in the past led to assertions from various parties that extrajudicial forces are influencing the interpretation of labor law in the state.

The rules that dictate such interorganizational actions are called institutions by economic sociologists. The actions of the ALRB, grower and labor interests, and any other organizations with which they regularly interact in an organizational field lead to the development of institutional frameworks. These institutional frameworks serve as a relatively malleable context for the behavior of organizations. In Scott's (2008) view, "Institutions are comprised of regulative, normative, and cultural-cognitive elements that, together with associated activities and resources, provide stability and meaning in social life" (p. 48). These rules, norms, and meanings constrain and enable organizational behavior. They can do so because of formal and informal sanctioning powers that grant them authority and legitimacy. Formal rules may be codified into law, the violation of which may create legal repercussions. This regulative dimension of institutions is normally associated with the state because it is usually states that have the power to create and enforce legal sanctions. Norms can be morally binding informally via social obligation. According to Scott (2008), norms define goals and objectives and provide socially appropriate means of obtaining them. Following, I explain in greater detail how this has worked historically and in the contemporary era with respect to farm labor mobilization. First, I provide a fuller understanding of institutions.

The notion of institutions that I employ relates to that introduced by "neo-institutionalists," who consider interorganizational rules and practices to be rituals. Drawing on Durkheim, these scholars emphasize the ritualistic elements of social structures and their ability to create and reinforce symbolic meanings (Meyer and Rowan 1977). From their perspective, institutions are simply sets of cultural rules.[1] Thus, Paul DiMaggio and Walter Powell (1983) are able to explain how stability and conformity emerge in fields even when some dynamism may be advantageous. They write, "Once a set of organizations emerges as a field, a paradox arises: rational actors make their organizations increasingly similar as they try to change them" (p. 147).

DiMaggio and Powell introduce three "isomorphic processes" to explain how this paradox emerges. They draw on Amos Hawley's (1968) description of the term and define isomorphism as a "constraining process that forces one unit in a population to resemble other units that face the same set of environmental conditions" (1983: 149). The process of coercive isomorphism leads to change when organizations feel pressured—by those who control resources they need—to alter their practices. Coercive isomorphism occurs, for instance, when a college is required by the federal government to institutionalize an institutional review board (IRB) before gaining access to federal research funds. Mimetic isomorphism, by contrast, occurs when organizations model their actions on those of other, more successful organizations. Normative isomorphism occurs when organizations in a particular field adopt widespread practices. These examples show how institutions serve as cultural expectations and normative constraints that bring about conformity and stability in organizational fields. Organizations not only gain legitimacy by conforming to dominant expectations and behaviors; they also become organizational actors capable of achieving their objectives. The Comité was exhibiting coercive isomorphism when it attempted to formalize so that it could more effectively navigate the institutions within its organizational field.

The development and application of institutions within fields may be further explained through Fligstein's discussion of markets as a particular type of field. For markets to function effectively, they require the production of stable social institutions such as laws and regulations. To produce market stability, governments, labor, and capital interests must come together to produce institutional arrangements. Fligstein explains how rules are developed and how they then structure relations among the actors in the field. This process can be applied to any field of competing and allied collective interests, including agriculture.

Prior to the implementation of the ALRA as an institutional framework to adjudicate farm labor conflict, labor mobilization in California was contentious, disruptive, and sometimes violent. Between 1965 and 1975, the UFW battled not only growers but also the rival Teamsters union as the UFW attempted to organize grape and lettuce workers. In 1966, for example, the UFW decided to launch a campaign to organize the DiGorgio Fruit Corporation, a large grape grower in the Central Valley. DiGorgio promptly responded that its workers were already covered by a contract with the Teamsters. The UFW protested in reply that workers' wishes had not been taken into account. As Philip Martin notes, however, "Since farm workers were not covered by federal or state labor laws, there was no need for an election to determine if workers wanted to be represented by the UFW or Teamsters" (2003: 68). Without formal mechanisms to adjudicate such disputes, the competing parties were forced to rely on ad-hoc solutions. Martin (2003) writes that clergy, politicians, and other labor leaders recommended that the American Arbitration Association oversee an election at DiGorgio.[2]

The UFW and the Teamsters continued to butt heads over unionization in the agriculture industry. In 1970 the UFW attempted to organize lettuce workers in the Salinas Valley. Once again, growers entered into talks with the Teamsters to avoid having to negotiate with the UFW. Such "sweetheart contracts" would have been illegal under the National Farm Labor Relations Act (Mooney and Majka 1995), but farmworkers were not covered by existing labor law. Violence ensued between the two unions. The Teamsters were accused of union busting when they brought in burly men to intimate UFW supporters. On several occasions fights broke out as rival picketers confronted each other on rural roads. It was during this time that UFW attorney Jerry Cohen was beaten and hospitalized (Mooney and Majka 1995). In 1973 Salinas Valley growers persuaded local judges to prevent the UFW from picketing on their operations because, according to the growers, workers were already under contract with the Teamsters. Thirty-two-hundred UFW picketers were arrested that year (Martin 2003). Without established and respected legal protections such as those that might be found in an institutional framework to adjudicate labor disputes, the UFW had great difficulty compelling growers to negotiate with workers in good faith.

The introduction of the ALRA demonstrates how incumbents, challengers, and the state create stable markets, and how these markets reproduce themselves on the basis of their rules. As shared assumptions, rules—formal or informal ones—introduce stability to interactions because they allow actors to form reasonable expectations about the actions of others. Since actors cannot govern themselves and do not have the authority to make rules binding, states are needed to implement and enforce a market's rules. So, for example, the tremendous amount of violence that occurred in the pre-ALRA era of farm labor mobilization can be attributed in part to the lack of an institutional regime, including formal sanctions, to guide the conduct of organizational actors in the agricultural field.

Institutions like the ALRA emerge when collective actors such as labor unions and growers' groups coordinate and compete with one another within organizational fields as they attempt to gain the favor of the state. It is therefore important to take into account the varying amounts of power that different organizational actors bring to a field and how these power differences influence the implementation of rules and laws, which in turn affect whose interests dominate within the field. Charles Perrow (1986) argued that organizations can wield tremendous social power. That power is based on organizational capacity, which in turn allows for the successful implementation of institutional strategies. In a field comprising the Comité, the UFW, the ALRB, and the Coastal Berry Company, among others, it is not difficult to ascertain which groups wielded greater institutional leverage. This knowledge and awareness of institutions is not unlike other resources available to organizations.

Institutions and organizations are homologous to cultures and individual actors. Consider a well-known passage from Clifford Geertz: "Man is a social animal suspended in webs of significance he himself has spun, I take culture to be these webs" (1973: 5). Now, return to Weber's description of organizations: "The management of an office follows general rules that are more or less stable, more or less exhaustive, and *which can be learned*" (quoted in Gerth and Mills 1946; emphasis mine). Learned behavior in organizations is homologous to culture from the perspective of individual social actors. Within and among organizations, institutions constitute Weber's learned behavior. When organizations act isomorphically in their dealings with other groups, they become socialized with particular behaviors that may allow them to meet their objectives in an appropriate manner. In this way knowledge of institutions held by organizations is analogous to the concept of cultural capital.

Cultural capital is usually described as a set of intangible traits possessed by an individual that function as resources in specific social contexts. These assets may be knowledge, skills, tastes, or dispositions serving as resources that individuals may leverage for personal gain. Similarly, awareness of relevant institutions provides an organization with the ability to pursue its interests. For the Comité, this capacity could have taken the form of understanding effective forms of engagement with other organizations, knowledge of administrative law, or access to the media or organizational networks.

The concept of discourse helps to further explain how cultural capital operates at the organizational level. Discourse may be defined as formal, generally accepted forms of communication used to organize and to adjudicate disputes. Scholars have argued that formal, rationalist discourse as a means of engagement in the public arena is itself a cultural product (Dryzek et al. 2003). If this is the case, then it must be learned; its interpretation and application may require a skilled practitioner. In this manner discourse can serve as a barrier to entry in the public arena while knowledge of formal discourse may facilitate the advancement of a group's interests. When the Comité elevated Sergio Leal and Jose Guadalupe Fernández to leadership positions because of their English language skills, they were in a very real way acknowledging their awareness of the kind of cultural capital needed to press their case.

The dynamic whereby marginalized groups such as farmworkers must first learn the rules of the game before they can successfully press their claims for social change can be viewed in historical events. Indeed, the Coastal Berry unionization campaign is better understood when situated historically, as a contemporary example of farm labor mobilization shaped by a long process of interactions among organizations including state regulatory agencies, for-profit firms, and a variety of labor and public-interest organizations. These various advocacy organizations and for-profit firms have a long history of interacting among one another to interpret and shape state and market structures in a manner advantageous to their agenda. To adequately assess labor conflict in California agriculture, it is thus necessary to understand the historical process that led to its formation.

Peter Berger and Thomas Luckmann tell us that "Institutions always have a history, of which they are the products" (1966: 54). Institutions are therefore the result of a historical process of contestation among allied and competing organizations. The historical process that led to the emergence of a legal framework for the adjudication of farm labor conflict in California is explored in the next section. A historical perspective on institutionalization is then expanded to explain why the earliest instances of farm labor mobilization in the state failed whereas collective action by contemporaneous ethnic-advocacy groups achieved some success. The historical data will demonstrate that marginalized groups must first establish themselves within organizational fields before they can create and manipulate institutional frameworks to affect social change.

The UFW and the ALRA

The implementation of the Agricultural Labor Relations Act in 1975, an institutional framework intended to adjudicate farm labor conflict, can be seen as the result of a process of contestation between the state, the UFW, and agricultural interests. Here, Fligstein's thinking is instructive. He writes about "the structuring of work in a society as the outcome of the political conflict between workers, government officials, and capitalists, and the labor market institutions they create" (2002: 101). Using a "historical institutional" theoretical framework compatible with the one employed here, Miriam Wells and Don Villarejo (2004) explain the development and declining efficacy of the ALRB. They conclude that public policies are the product of mutually constitutive processes among state and societal actors: "While in this case class-based organizations helped shape the form and impacts of state institutions, those institutions themselves set the conditions for class organizing and political contestation and structured the conditions for political success" (2004: 292–293).

Wells and Villarejo use the term *class capacity* to describe the ability of capital and labor interests to influence the political process and shape the institutional framework for the adjudication of labor disputes. They evaluate the activities of the UFW and the agriculture industry in California in the periods preceding and following the implementation of the ALRA and determine that it was a shift in union strategy, as opposed to external political conditions, that led to the first and sharpest decline in the efficacy of the ALRA after 1977–1978. Their analysis draws attention to the ways in which collective actors shape their organizational field or environment, just as organizations are in turn influenced by environmental conditions. Not only does the state structure social movement outcomes, but also social movements themselves influence state institutions that set the parameters for social movement behavior. Wells and Villarejo note, "The production of social change requires not only an institutional apparatus, but a set of social relations that alter power. Here the strategies of insurgent groups make a difference" (2004: 318).

Marshall Ganz (2000) turns to differences in the strategies of insurgent groups to explain the success of the UFW between 1959 and 1966. He revisits an old question in social movement theory and finds the conventional answer provided by Jenkins and Perrow (1977) to be lacking. That question is, Why was the UFW able to succeed when other farm labor organizations failed? Ganz argues that the focus on political opportunity structure offered by Jenkins and Perrow is insufficient. He writes, "Understanding social movements, however, requires accounting for the fact that different actors act in different ways, some of which influence their environments more than others. Some see political opportunities where others do not, mobilize resources in ways others do not, and frame their causes in ways that others do not (2000: 1009).

Ganz uses the concept of *strategic capacity* to explain the likelihood that organizations will be able to develop effective strategies.[3] Strategic capacity is based on three factors: access to salient information, employment of heuristic processes, and deep motivation on the part of leaders. Strategic capacity allows organizations to achieve positive outcomes, according to Ganz (2000). In its infancy, the UFW was able to develop a strategic capacity that allowed it to overcome an organizational "liability of newness," a phrase Ganz borrows from Stinchcombe, to succeed as a farm labor organization. Ganz writes, "As students of 'street smarts' have long understood, 'resourcefulness' can sometimes compensate for lack of resources. While learning how the environment influences actors is very important, learning more about how actors influence the environment is the first step not only to understanding the world, but to changing it" (2000: 1044).

The complementary perspectives of Ganz (2000) and Wells and Villarejo (2004) call attention to the actions of organizational actors on their environment, especially the state, as these actors attempt to shape that environment so that it is structured in a way advantageous to the achievement of organizational objectives. A closer look at the historical record reveals that only when marginalized groups have achieved a sufficient degree of organizational capacity can they influence their environments in such a manner.

In the sections that follow, this theoretical framework is used to explain the historical emergence of Mexican American political participation in California and the Southwest during the first half of the twentieth century. This approach shows how strategic engagement with established institutional frameworks can facilitate social change. The discussion then turns to a brief history of farmworker mobilization in the state during the 1930s. In contrast to more urban-based political groups, farmworkers were unable to mobilize successfully, and their inability to engage prevailing institutional forms explains why. If institutions are based on habitualization, as Berger and Luckmann (1966) tell us, then it is important to understand the historical patterns of interaction that led to the social and political integration of ethnic and labor advocacy groups. As I explain below, the UFW, like previous successful organizations, was able to bring about social change only by learning the rules of the game and working within established institutional frameworks to meet its objectives.

The twin histories of Mexican American political advocacy and farm labor mobilization in the western United States can be understood in terms of the organizational acquisition, development, and exercise of institutional knowledge in an attempt to bring about social change. The UFW thus can be seen as the organizational successor to earlier Mexican American civil rights and workers' groups in the region. It was the first Mexican American farm labor organization to employ a political and legal component in its efforts to engender social change. While Mexican American organizations in the Southwest (many of which were primarily middle-class groups) had successfully engaged prevailing political institutions, until the emergence of the UFW in 1964, farm labor groups had not done so. This institutional engagement made the UFW highly successful in its efforts, whereas previous attempts to change the lot of farmworkers usually met with limited outcomes.

Mexican American Political Advocacy in California and the Southwest

The emergence in the 1960s of the UFW and other ethnic-based political action groups is predicated on the long history of Mexican American political mobilization dating to the early part of the twentieth century in the Southwest. Refuting claims by ethnic historians that political activity among Mexican Americans began in earnest in the post–World War II period, Mario García (1989) presents a history of collective action for social justice by Mexican Americans beginning in the 1930s. Drawing on the works of Mannheim and other social scientists, García proposes the concept of a political generation to explain the first wave of significant civil rights organizing among Mexican-origin people in the United States. During the 1930s there occurred a reorientation of loyalties and aspirations among the Mexican-origin population away from Mexico and toward the United States. This cultural realignment had significant implications for the way in which this group organized and pressed claims for social change.

According to George Sánchez (1993), it is during the 1930s that a Mexican American identity first began to emerge in the country. He points to decreased immigration from Mexico and deportation and repatriation programs, both caused by the onset of the Great Depression, as major factors in the consolidation of a Mexican American community. From 1930 to 1935, Los Angeles lost one-third of its Mexican-origin population (Sánchez 1993). Sánchez notes that those who remained were keenly aware of their second-class status, and they formed the base of a new community for whom culture was the basis of political participation during the New Deal era to follow. This generation assumed a dual identity, became socialized to the promises of American democracy, and fought for full inclusion into American society by employing strategies appropriate for the institutional settings of the time. The process by which these Mexican Americans assumed a bicultural identity and organized to ensure their equal standing in American society has been well chronicled by social historians.[4] This history demonstrates a clear understanding of American political structures and the use of institutional strategies in efforts that succeeded in bringing about social change.

The League of United Latin American Citizens (LULAC) was the first major organization to embody a hybrid identity and embrace mainstream institutional processes in its political advocacy work. The group was founded in1929 by mostly middle-class Mexican American Texans. During the 1930s and 1940s, LULAC created self-sustaining local chapters throughout Texas, New Mexico, Arizona, Kansas, and California. These chapters were active in local politics and supported Hispanic and Hispanic-friendly politicians. The organization's willingness to embrace established institutional structures differentiated it from other contemporaneous ethnic political advocacy groups.

In its efforts to bring about social change, the organization sought to "promote and develop among LULAC members what they called the 'best and purest' form of Americanism" (Gutiérrez 1995: 77). The organization was intent on demonstrating its American qualities; it conducted its proceedings in English, prominently displayed the American flag at meetings and on its stationary, and recited the "George Washington prayer" at the beginning of meetings (Gutiérrez 1995). This behavior exemplifies mimetic isomorphism whereby organizations adapt the norms and behaviors of other successful organizations. In the case of LULAC these efforts were also meant to demonstrate a cultural similarity with the mainstream, which at the time was overwhelmingly white.

Some scholars have labeled LULAC's model of social activism "assimilationist" or "integrationist" (Márquez 2003; Gutiérrez 1995). These terms refer to the organization's willingness to take on a mainstream identity while shunning an overly ethnic character. A closer look, however, reveals a more nuanced reality. The group was successful in its work for the empowerment of Mexican Americans as citizens precisely because it appropriated an organizational culture and structure that resonated with other state entities and civic groups in its organizational environment just as I have described above. Furthermore, by focusing its objectives on the achievement of the principles of equality and justice on which the country was founded, the organization was aligning itself with fundamental ideals in American political culture, thus making its goals more palatable to a wider range of organizations and individuals. While LULAC's approach may be construed as assimilationist, I argue that it only succeeded because it developed organizational capacity and institutional awareness.

Like LULAC, El Congreso de Pueblos de Habla Española (Congress of Spanish Speaking Peoples, or the Congress), was able to effectively work for social change by adapting conventional organizational principles and navigating the dominant political and social institutions of the era. Unlike LULAC, however, the Congress did not maintain that Mexican-origin people should assume a stronger American identity. The Congress was started in 1938 as a coalition of labor and community groups organized to fight oppression. Drawing its constituency primarily from the working class, the Congress emphasized labor organizing as the basis for social change. Its platform stressed, "The Trade Union Movement provides the most basic agency through which the Mexican and Spanish Speaking people become organized" (in Sánchez 1993: 247). The Congress also engaged in a broad range of political activities and actively sought support from liberal-minded elites in the entertainment industry and politics. As a coalition, the group demonstrated a sophisticated ability to work within an organizational field and align with groups with similar interests to wield greater institutional leverage as it pressed its claims for social change.

Regardless of their class composition and cultural orientations, Mexican American organizations through the period leading up to World War II were knowledgeable about existing institutional arrangements and adept at navigating complex organizational fields as they worked to achieve their goals. According to David Gutiérrez, "LULAC leaders seemed to believe that the essential challenge facing the Mexican American people was to develop and employ a political strategy that would enable them to organize most effectively for the achievement of meaningful social change" (1995: 82). But, other organizations that did not share LULAC's assimilationist position were guided by a similar principle. The more working class–oriented Congress successfully courted local and state politicians to support its civil rights advocacy efforts. During this time, LULAC, the Congress, and other civil rights organizations actively participated in the political process by engaging in electoral politics, encouraging Mexican Americans to run for public office, endorsing candidates, and building coalitions with similar organizations. According to Sánchez (1993), the increase in political activity within the Mexican American community during the 1930s and 1940s was the result of a desire for increased integration into American society. This engagement with politics via formal institutional processes differentiated Mexican American civil rights organizations of the 1930s from labor organizations of the same period.

Farm Labor Mobilization in California

US farm-labor insurgency rose dramatically in the 1930s. In California, strikes and other large-scale work actions took place in the greater Los Angeles area, the Central San Joaquin Valley, and the Imperial Valley in the south.[5] There were dozens of strikes, work stoppages, organizing efforts, and other acts of mobilization for social change around farm labor. The largest strike ever in the American agricultural industry, for example, occurred in the San Joaquin Valley in 1933 and involved well over 10,000 workers, at least 75 percent of whom were Mexican (González 1999). Despite widespread labor mobilization, labor unions were unable to significantly alter social conditions due to their inability to engage state institutions or the broader political system. A brief analysis of labor activity during this period helps explain why.

An examination of early farm labor activity in California reveals the complex relationships among the various groups that formed the organizational field of labor mobilization and highlights the social and political marginalization of farm workers. US and Mexican governmental agencies at the local, state, and federal levels played an active role in these early struggles. The grower community was also intimately involved and well organized into various lobbying groups to ensure that their economic interests were served in the political arena. Their efforts were usually successful: the state often acted in favor of the growers. During this era the Mexican government was known to intervene in labor disputes, usually working in conjunction with political and economic elites in the United States to curb the militancy of Mexican workers in the North (González 1999). We see here the effective navigation of an existing organizational field by a variety of collective actors *except farmworkers*.

Organized labor was also a part of the farmworker struggles of the 1930s, but labor did not share the organizational cohesion or political clout of the growers. Each union had its own set of concerns and goals, and these did not always coincide with the needs and aspirations of the farmworkers themselves. Conflicts of interest also existed within the Mexican community. The historical record shows that middle-class Mexican social organizations were often unwilling to support the Mexican laboring masses (González 1999; Gutiérrez 1995). Farmworkers attempting to organize at this time were the one set of participants in the mobilization field who lacked the ability to court influential allies or gain access to the political process. Mexican-origin workers' limited gains reflected this critical inability to sustain organizational cohesion and wield political influence.

During the 1930s, farmworker labor insurgencies usually began with ethnic-based workers' groups emerging from the labor force working a particular crop in a particular area (Daniel 1981). Even when these spontaneous actions sometimes reached great numbers, they tended to be highly localized, often within a single growing region. Typically, they were also short lived and absent of full organizational coalescing. At most they lasted a harvesting season, but they often were much shorter than that because of the swift and severe repression methods of growers and law enforcement officials (Daniel 1981; L. Majka 1981). The short lifespan of these worker actions restricted the degree and type of mobilization and the objectives that could be pursued. Workers engaging in these actions usually made limited demands for wage increases or pressed for better working conditions. Their actions tended not to have broader social or political agendas (L. Majka 1981). Because of the restricted nature of these actions by loosely structured organizations, workers were constrained in their ability to bring about lasting change, either at the worksite or within the larger social environment.

A strategy open to farm laborers was to align themselves with more established labor unions to gain concessions from growers. However, established labor unions often had their own agendas when organizing farmworkers. According to Cletus Daniel, "Each resolved to advance its own special interests by organizing the state's previously neglected farm-labor force. What was never quite so plain was just what advantages would accrue to the workers themselves as a consequence of the exertions on their behalf by these outside labor organizations" (1981: 76). In the early 1900s, for example, the Industrial Workers of the World (IWW, also known as the Wobblies) sought to provide all workers with an anticapitalist alternative to what its members saw as an accommodating craft unionism in the American Federation of Labor. As such, it was imperative to organize California's large agriculture workforce, lest farmworkers undermine the Wobblies' movement. However, the IWW did not negotiate or administer contracts as a traditional labor union (Majka 1981). Because it refused to engage in accepted institutional practices of the time, the IWW was unable to significantly alter the conditions of farm labor in the state.

Another group interested in the state's farmworkers was the communist Agricultural Workers Industrial League (AWIL), which became active in the mid-1930s. Because of the group's ideological position, it was marginalized by mainstream unions whose help it attempted to enlist, and its organizers were subject to strong governmental repression. Association with organizations considered communist or otherwise radical ultimately harmed the cause of the farmworkers. These organizations and their members were subject to harsh censure from the state. More important, they lacked the organization and political connections of either growers or mainstream labor unions and therefore had a difficult time pressing their agendas in the political realm.

Farmworker mobilization during this early period followed a particular pattern. When farmworkers organized themselves, they usually had great difficulty achieving success; when their demands were met, they were often limited in time and scope. If workers chose to align themselves with outside organizations, they were still marginalized and vulnerable to repression because of their relationships to groups considered radical. During this time, farmworkers were isolated and unable, on their own or through alliances, to develop and sustain the organizational capacity necessary to engage the political system and thus engender meaningful social change. This inability suggests that to bring about substantive social change, collective actors must be sufficiently organized and institutionally knowledgeable to sustain engagement with a wide variety of organizations across multiple social and political fields. This review of farmworker mobilization in the first three decades of the twentieth century reveals failure to do so.

The Emergence of the UFW

It would take until the 1960s for farm labor advocates to succeed in obtaining major improvements in farmworker welfare. Certain social and political institutional preconditions had to be met before the UFW could fully emerge as an active and successful organization. As many scholars of Mexican American social history have noted, World War II significantly curtailed the nascent civil rights activities of the Mexican American community. Some organizations such as LULAC went into a period of dormancy. Others, like the Congress, dissipated. For organizations working on behalf of farmworkers, the 1940s and 1950s were particularly difficult.

The institutional context for labor mobilization from 1942 to 1964 was the Bracero Program, which was a state-sponsored and - administered system of temporary labor importation for the American agriculture industry. The Bracero Program demonstrates the way in which coordinated efforts by well-organized groups can succeed in "capturing the state" and in doing so persuade the state to act in the interest of those actors. This can, however, cause problems for the state. Kitty Calavita (1992) uncovers the "structural contradictions" that emerge when state bureaucracies and institutions are influenced in different ways, depending on their location within the state apparatus. She shows that the US Congress disavowed its control over the controversial issues of immigration and labor by bestowing the Immigration and Naturalization Service (INS) with such powers. The job of the INS was in essence to handle the dual and contradictory task of controlling illegal immigration while ensuring that growers had "a seemingly endless army of cheap, unorganized workers" (Calavita 1992: 9).

Not surprisingly, farm labor mobilization during the 1940s and 1950s was limited by the Bracero Program's importation of Mexican laborers to work in the agriculture industry. Farm labor advocacy during this period focused its efforts not on the agriculture industry itself but on legislation in an effort to alter existing institutional arrangements. One of the most notable figures of the farm labor movement during this time was Ernesto Galarza. In 1942, while working on his PhD in economics at Columbia University, Galarza first came into contact with the Bracero Program. He wrote a report in which he characterized the relationship between US. agriculture and Mexican *braceros* as an exploitative one. In 1946 Galarza went to California to work for the National Farm Labor Union. His involvement in various strikes in California and Louisiana led him to realize that there were several major impediments to organizing farmworkers.

Besides the indifference of organized labor and the anti-farmworker position of local and state authorities, Galarza realized that the Bracero Program and the influx of illegal Mexican labor made labor organizing nearly impossible. The Bracero Program was, in his eyes, the most pernicious of these formidable obstacles. He wrote, "I made up my mind that, until the law was changed, I would never again ask a farm worker to stick his neck out when it could be chopped off by one stroke of a pen—a pen held in the hand of some bureaucrat in San Francisco or Washington, D.C.—certifying more braceros" (in London and Anderson 1970: 124).

In 1956 Galarza published a book titled *Strangers in Our Fields* that documents the abuses of the Bracero Program. It received widespread attention. Galarza was able to garner the support of a wide variety of urban liberal, church, and other civic groups to repeal Public Law 78, which had authorized the program. In the late 1950s and early 1960s, public pressure escalated. In 1964, Congress rescinded authorization to renew the program.

The Bracero Program is an excellent example of public policy as an institution. Here, agribusiness advocacy groups were successful in lobbying the federal government to codify and administer a system of labor importation that benefited their collective interests. Growers were successful in their efforts because their organizational capacity and institutional awareness were far greater than that of the less organized farmworkers. Farm labor advocates succeeded in having the law rescinded only when they were able to convince other like-minded organizations of their cause and thus wield the political leverage necessary to dismantle the institution of government-sponsored and - administered labor importation.

The end of the Bracero Program signaled a new institutional environment in which Mexican American farm labor mobilization was to take place. Although farm laborers in California had been organizing since the first decades of the twentieth century, it is only in the mid-1960s that they were sufficiently organized to engage other collective actors, whether allies or antagonists, and affect institutional arrangements in society. The repeal of the Bracero Program impressed upon farm labor advocates the importance of the political process for labor mobilization. Even though better-organized and more institutionally savvy, urban Mexican American political advocacy groups had long used the political system to their advantage—before the 1960s farm laborers had been unable to do so. The UFW was the first rural working-class organization to use political and legal strategies effectively. It developed an organizational capacity that allowed it to successfully engage institutional processes to achieve its goals of economic and social equality. This configuration was unique among Mexican American social movement organizations at the time.[6]

Ethnic Identity and Mobilization

Previously, I stated that all Mexican American advocacy groups have had to contend with the dual issues of cultural orientation and institutional engagement. These themes are mirrored in the larger civil rights movement of the 1960s. Disenfranchised groups working to achieve equality, particularly ethnic minorities, also had to contend with issues of collective identity and institutional strategy. Like African Americans, Mexican Americans had to articulate some sort of identity based on both the dominant American society and their own cultural heritage. Many organizations adopted a self-consciously oppositional sense of identity and celebrated their difference from mainstream American society. Other groups chose not to emphasize cultural difference in overt ways. Civil rights groups also had to decide whether they accepted the fundamental nature of American society and wished to work within the system toward full and complete integration or work to undermine or otherwise separate themselves from the system. Organizations at this time varied widely in their positions on these two issues.

In this regard the UFW was innovative when it first emerged as an ethnic working-class labor organization with a dynamic political and legal action component. Until the birth of the UFW, Mexican farm labor organizations had not been able to effectively engage the American political system.[7] The UFW differs in that it not only chose to make use of existing institutional arrangements, as had previous Mexican American civil rights organizations, but it did so while maintaining a strong sense of ethnic Chicano identity.

The UFW is further distinguished by its continuity as a formal organization and its use of institutional mechanisms to gain favorable legislation for California farmworkers. Important changes in the legal code spurred by UFW action have succeeded in making lasting improvements in overall working conditions for laborers in the state. These gains only came about, however, because the UFW was sufficiently organized to successfully maneuver among like-minded and antagonistic organizations to alter existing institutional arrangements to better serve the interests of farmworkers.

The success and survival of the UFW and other organizational vehicles of the disenfranchised depended on their ability to harness institutional power, particularly in the legal arena. The NAACP has historically excelled at this sort of work.[8] The organization has been successful in furthering the cause of racial equality in the United States by employing legal strategies that altered fundamental institutions in American society. Such strategies presuppose a sophisticated organizational capacity that includes skilled officials, such as attorneys, who have an intimate understanding of the law. American jurisprudence is itself a major social institution that functions as the ultimate rule book by which social change occurs. The NAACP's use of legal strategies demonstrates a clear understanding that substantive social change in complex societies comes about only by altering existing institutional arrangements. The 1954 *Brown v. the Board of Education* decision outlawing *de jure* segregation and the repeal of the Bracero Program are two excellent examples of social change via institutional processes.

Like the NAACP, LULAC has consistently worked for social change by shaping existing institutional arrangements. In this regard, in the Mexican American community LULAC can be considered a precursor to the UFW.[9] What these three groups share is an emphasis on legal and political strategies as mechanisms for social change. Today, both LULAC and the UFW are active participants in local, state, and national politics—they are effective organizational actors in their respective organizational fields.

On the eve of the strawberry campaign in the late 1990s, the UFW found itself heir to a long tradition of successful mobilization via formal institutional channels on behalf of ethnic minority and farm labor groups. The organization was well equipped and institutionally adept as it exercised its agency in multiple organizational spheres. As the historical record presented here demonstrates, it is only when marginalized groups develop sufficiently robust organizational structures that they are able to engage the institutional foundations of the US political system to bring about lasting structural change.

The office that I had difficulty finding in September 2000 is clear evidence of this hard-won ability to engage with powerful organizations through existing institutions. Through their coordinated efforts, the UFW and its allies in state and civil society helped to give birth to the ALRA and the ALRB in 1975, permanently changing the balance of power between labor and agribusiness in California. With the new labor legislation, the UFW managed to do what no other farm labor union had accomplished: it went beyond winning a skirmish here and there to changing the rules of the game governing labor conflict in the organizational field of agriculture. The ALRA, while not always effective, is the successful outcome of a push for legitimacy by the state's farmworkers. It is a testament to the power of organizations and institutions in society.

---

[1] A similar argument is made by Sharon Hayes (1994), who contends that culture can enable and constrain actors in much the same way that social structures do.

[2] DiGorgio reluctantly agreed to the election, which the UFW won in 1967. However, a year later, in 1968, DiGorgio went out of business (Martin 2003).

[3] The careful reader may note a similarity between Ganz's concept of strategic capacity and my own concept of organizational capacity. My concept of organizational capacity is a broader term used to refer to an organization's ability to effectively navigate its organizational field.

[4] See González 1999; Gutiérrez 1995; Sánchez 1993; García 1989.

[5] For a more extensive discussion of labor mobilization during the 1930s, see Daniel 1981; González 1999; and L. Majka 1981.

[6] A well-known article by Jenkins and Perrow (1977) holds as its thesis that the UFW was able to achieve success where previous farmworkers' movements had not because of the latter union's engagement with the political system. But the UFW's political engagement is less remarkable when one considers the history of political mobilization by Mexican-descent civil rights organizations in the United States.

[7] There had, however, been labor-based social service organizations among the Mexican workforce. Notable examples are the *Mutualista* organizations that were prevalent among Mexican immigrants fleeing the political and social upheaval of the Mexican Revolution. These precursors of the UFW were community-based mutual aid associations that provided members with services such as funeral insurance and credit unions (Márquez 2003). What distinguishes these groups from the UFW, with which they shared a common purpose, was their notion of themselves as *Mexicanos de Afuera*, Mexicans from outside the country (Márquez 2003; García 1989). They thought of themselves principally as Mexican and saw their time in the United States as temporary. Thus, they did not seek lasting social change through political participation.

[8] See McAdam (1982) for an extended discussion of the NAACP before, during, and after the civil rights movement era.

[9] LULAC continues to be one of the most prominent Latino advocacy groups in the United States. In recent decades LULAC has developed relationships to US corporate philanthropists including Anheuser-Busch, Coca-Cola Company, and Iowa Beef Producers (IBP). As a labor union, the UFW has not developed similar relationships with corporate sponsors.

8

Incorporating Immigrants into an Organization Society

As I have shown, the UFW was able to win a union contract at the Coastal Berry Company despite stiff resistance from farmworkers in the company's fields. The concepts of social networks, formal organizations, and institutions help to reveal that it was the UFW's organizational capacity that facilitated an institutional awareness that in turn enabled it to overcome the strength of interpersonal bonds among workers at the Coastal Berry Company. But, what are the larger social implications of this case? What does this story of failure and success in farm labor organization at the nexus of incipient and established organization and governmental institutions mean for farmworkers, Mexican immigrants, and American society as a whole?

As one of the most difficult and lowest-paid occupations, farmwork almost invariably benefits from unionization. In this case, a more unsettling corollary argument can also be made. Whatever worksite improvements that may have occurred at the Coastal Berry Company came at the expense of potential immigrant empowerment and social incorporation.[1] This bold and perhaps perplexing claim begins to make sense if we recall the manner in which the UFW was able to wrest control from the Comité, even though that nascent group enjoyed strong support among workers. As stated in the previous chapter, the UFW was able to score a victory not because it won the hearts and minds of workers but rather because it had superior organizational capacity and institutional awareness.

As a formal organization with a sophisticated understanding of institutional arrangements, the UFW has been highly successful in its efforts to bring about meaningful social changes that have improved the lives of farmworkers in the United States. However, in recent years the UFW has been less successful at facilitating the incorporation of these same immigrants into American society. The same complex organizational structure that allows the UFW to successfully press claims for immigrants also inhibits the meaningful participation of those immigrants in the union. As mentioned in Chapter 5, the UFW has become a professional social movement organization. According to Mayer Zald and John McCarthy, rank-and-file members in these organizations have limited avenues for meaningful participation and "no serious role in organizational policymaking short of withholding membership dues. The professional staff largely determines the positions the organization takes upon issues" (1987: 378). Lack of participation by farmworkers in their own organization has troubling implications for the incorporation of immigrants into mainstream society. As one of the few large-scale social advocacy organizations to work with immigrants, the UFW could serve as a much more effective vehicle for immigrants' civic incorporation. The organization has unfortunately proven limited in this regard. If one values the successful incorporation of immigrants into American society through meaningful participation in civic organizations, the case of the strawberry campaign should be cause for concern.

Organizations function as schools of democracy, where immigrants learn about public issues and develop the civic and political skills necessary to be actively engaged citizens. This process of socialization develops stakeholders with a sense of belonging and community in their new society. Arguments along these lines have been made persuasively by Putnam (2000), Ramakrishnan and Bloemraad (2008), Skocpol (2003), and Wong (2006). Unfortunately, the UFW has developed in a way that minimizes this dimension of the organization. The meaningful incorporation of immigrants into its organizational structure has not been a primary concern of the group. This lack of social incorporating has not kept the UFW from successfully advocating for the rights of workers and improving the lot of immigrants in the United States. Nevertheless, the UFW has served this function in the past, and as a labor union it continues to be a logical vehicle for immigrant incorporation into American society. The Comité and similar groups can, by contrast, serve in this capacity. Unfortunately, that group was pressed out of existence when its organizational interests ran counter to those of the more established and better organized UFW. This contest between immigrants and organized labor has significant implications for the way US democracy works. If large professional organizations remain the dominant civic and political actors in society, there will be fewer new, less formal organizations whose members can be effective political agents, and any such organizations are less able to facilitate the incorporation of the newest members of society into the mainstream.[2] The implications of the Coastal Berry case for the incorporation of immigrants into American society are addressed in this concluding chapter. To properly situate this discussion, it is necessary to first review the historical development of the UFW's organizational structure and identity from the time of Cesar Chavez to its current form as a union with limited avenues of grassroots participation. Once this organizational history has been presented, the work of political theorist Theda Skocpol enters to explain the emergence of professional organizations that since the 1960s have proven detrimental to the civic health of American society. I then apply Skocpol's theory to the Coastal Berry case, for which her argument is expanded to consider implications for immigrants in the United States.

The UFW's Organizational Structure and Identity

The UFW has made impressive gains as a politically active, ethnically based labor organization. However, the organizational capacity necessary to sustain its multidimensional efforts has developed and expanded at the expense of its labor organizing efforts. An unintended consequence has been a decreased role for farmworkers in the administrative apparatus of the organization. To appreciate this argument, one must consider the origins and historical trajectory of the organization. The union was founded in 1962 by Cesar Chavez, who originally envisioned a farm labor–based social service and advocacy group with a broad range of goals for political and economic justice. Organizing a community on the basis of its labor was the vehicle used by the organization to bring about social change. However, the group was not originally conceived as a labor organization in the narrow sense of the term. It was only in 1965, when it joined forces with the AFL-CIO–affiliated Filipino Agricultural Workers Organizing Committee (AWOC), that the organization explicitly functioned as a farm labor union. Even then, the union maintained its commitment to social change for Mexican American workers outside the narrow scope of the worksite.

Over time, the UFW has evolved into a political advocacy group that is highly effective in its efforts to bring about social change in formal institutional arenas. However, political and legal activity by a group whose primary objective is ostensibly to organize farmworkers demands a complex organizational structure with a highly trained staff. This demand has led the UFW to develop into an organization of skilled professionals minimally reliant on the participation of farmworkers. As the UFW became increasingly involved in institutional politics, its labor organizing activities in the fields has diminished. The meaningful participation of farmworkers in the union's leadership likewise decreased. This decreased democratic participation can be traced to two of the union's most impressive gains: the highly successful grape boycott of the late 1960s and the 1975 passage of the Agricultural Labor Relations Act (ALRA). These related achievements were the most significant events in the UFW's early history and shaped the organization's current structure and identity.

In 1968 the UFW launched a dramatically successful boycott against the entrenched California grape industry. With the support of labor leaders and civil rights, student, and environmental organizations, the union established boycott committees in fifty to sixty cities in the United States (Mooney and Majka 1995). As the strength of the boycott became apparent, the union moved organizers out of the fields and into urban centers to run boycott committees (Bardacke 1997, 2011). According to Frank Bardacke, however, this shift in effort had an unintended consequence as "the boycott tail came to wag the farm worker dog" (1993: 131). The removal of the UFW's organizers from the fields left a significant void in the union's field organizing efforts. Jerry Cohen, the UFW's first general council, made a similar argument in a 1986 letter to the *Los Angeles Times* titled "[The] UFW Must Get Back to Organizing." In the letter, Cohen writes that "given the current resources of the UFW, the boycott may be a necessary response to the situation. But it is not sufficient to change deteriorating conditions in the fields.... Only day-to-day organizing by the farm workers' union can help these people assert their legal rights in an effective manner" (Cohen 1986). Both Bardacke and Cohen point to the fact that during the 1970s and 1980s the UFW increasingly turned its attention away from the fields and focused on the grape boycott as the most important component in its arsenal of tactics.

The successful passage of the ALRA in 1975 further expanded the UFW's institutional efforts in the political and legal arenas. During the early 1970s, the union continued to grow as a participant in institutional politics by fighting court cases to set legal precedent for social change, submitting amicus briefs, and canvassing for Democratic candidates. However, the ALRA changed the nature of the UFW's legal-political participation. The act had profound implications for the UFW in that it altered the organizational structure of the group and changed its tactics. The legislation quickly forced the union much further into legal and political organizational fields. Almost immediately, the UFW had to redirect its attention to legal issues surrounding the new legislation. Union work now involved winning representative elections and negotiating contracts under the procedural guidelines established by the act. According to Theo and Linda Majka, "All this would require a more formalized union structure with specialized positions" (Majka and Majka 1992: 13). One important outcome was the expansion of the organization's legal staff to fight increasingly common court battles.

A change in organizational structure as a result of shifting institutional frameworks is not unique to the UFW. Other advocacy organizations have faced the same issue. An excellent example of similar phenomenon can be found in Suzanne Staggenborg's (1991) study of the pro-choice movement after the landmark 1973 Supreme Court ruling *Roe v. Wade,* which legalized abortion in the United States. In her study, Staggenborg analyzes the changes that took place within the movement in response to the newly passed legislation. The pro-choice movement assumed a greater formalized structure, and its attention shifted away from grassroots activities to the legal arena as it attempted to fend off legal challenges to abortion. In fighting these threats, the movement's tactics became more institutional and focused on legal-political processes. In the process NARAL (the National Association for the Repeal of Abortion Laws) and other pro-choice organizations began to behave like traditional interest groups and political insiders and less like the decentralized grassroots organizations they originally were (Staggenborg 1991). The pro-choice movement case is analogous to the case of the UFW after the 1975 passage of ALRA, as the work of farm labor advocacy increasingly moved out of the fields and into the courtrooms.

When the UFW's boycott activities and legal work as a political advocacy organization increased in the late 1970s and early 1980s, its labor organizing in the fields decreased. From July 1979 to June 1982, thirty-seven certification elections were held on average per year. From 1983 to 1985, the average diminished to twenty-nine elections per year. During the next three-year period, from 1985 to 1988, the annual average dropped further to seventeen elections per year (Mooney and Majka 1995). During this period of decline, the union's strength among farmworkers ebbed. As the UFW shifted its activities, it did not create the type of organizational structure that would have facilitated the democratic integration of the farmworker base into the administrative apparatus of the union (Bardacke 2011; Pawel 2009). Because the UFW never developed union locals, there were limited avenues for a rank-and-file worker to make it into the union leadership. Sidney Tarrow addresses this issue when he writes, "The problem for movement organizers is to create organizational models that are sufficiently robust to stand up to opponents, but flexible enough to change to new circumstances and draw on energies at the base" (1994: 136). Certainly this is not an easy task. Organizations need a constant infusion of grassroots participation to remain dynamic and viable entities for social change. This need was particularly pertinent in the case of the UFW, which drew its legitimacy as an organization from the farmworkers it was organizing. When farmworker participation waned, the UFW opened itself to criticism, even though it was still acting on behalf of the workers. Waning participation has also played out in the sometimes tense relationship between the UFW and the workers it seeks to organize.

The outcome of the UFW's internal strife between 1978 and 1981 highlights the lack of democratic procedures in the union.[3] The first instance of trouble occurred within the union leadership. In 1979 Chavez decided to move the union's headquarters to La Paz, California, a tiny town in the Tehachapi Mountains, about 2½ hours' drive southeast of Bakersfield and 3½ hours from Delano, where the union was first started. Chavez wanted to consolidate the union and refocus its activities. An important aspect of the move was the issue of whether staff workers should be paid. In an interview, chief legal counsel Jerry Cohen told me he had never liked the desolate UFW village of La Paz and had no desire to move his operation away from the centers of union activity around Salinas and the San Joaquin Valley (2000). Furthermore, Cohen insisted to Chavez that he and the legal staff needed at least a modest income to continue the massive dual task of labor legislation and contract negotiation and maintenance. Aware of the significance of a well-trained legal staff, Chavez proposed to Cohen that he train a legal staff of volunteers in La Paz. Cohen would be paid for his work and then be free to leave. Cohen objected to this arrangement because he did not think it was fair that he be paid for his labors while the staff was not. Unable to reconcile these differences, Cohen and most of the legal staff left the union in 1979. The departure of the legal staff and its talented director was a serious blow to the structural integrity of the union. Not only would the union thus have limited ability to negotiate and service contracts, it would also be hampered in its ability to use the legal system as a powerful mechanism for farm labor advocacy, a maneuver at which Cohen had been particularly adept. During this period other key members of the organization left, including Marshall Ganz, head organizer for fifteen years; Gilbert Padilla, a union founder and secretary treasurer; Jessica Govea, director of the union's health service program;

and Eliseo Medina, a member of the executive board (Majka and Majka 1992).

Two years later, the union experienced another internal struggle, this time among its rank-and-file workers. In the late 1970s, Salinas-area lettuce pickers wanted to continue a successful lettuce strike whereas Chavez and the union leadership wanted to end the strike and return to a boycott. These men, usually better paid than San Joaquin workers, exhibited a high degree of worker solidarity and did not always bow to Chavez and the union leadership (Majka and Majka 1992). Jerry Cohen has described the Salinas workers as autonomous, proud, and tightly knit crews of mostly single men who were different from the Chicano families the union first organized in the San Joaquin Valley vineyards (2000). A confrontation between these workers and the union leadership occurred in the UFW's annual convention in 1981. That year, a group of worker representatives from Salinas proposed a slate of officers different from that offered by the union's executive board. At issue was the degree of local autonomy workers should have from the union leadership. The representatives also wanted to have a greater say in the important decision-making procedures of the union. Of particular importance to the Salinas workers was that they have a say in the strategies used to win contracts in the lettuce fields. The union leadership favored a boycott, but the workers wanted a strike. At one point during the convention, top union leaders began to chant, "Boycott! Boycott!" to which worker representatives chanted "*¡Huelga! ¡Huelga!* [Strike! Strike!]" (Bardacke 2002, 2011). Through a series of procedural maneuvers, the workers were sidelined from the convention. Following the convention, steps were taken to remove the representatives from their positions of leadership. The workers sued the union, claiming that since they were elected by farmworkers they could not be fired from their positions by the union leadership. Although the workers won their case, it was a significant blow to farmworkers and the union alike. It signaled to workers that dissention would not be tolerated within the ranks (Bardacke 2002; Cohen 2000).[4]

The events of the late 1970s and early 1980s illustrate not only the centralization of power within the union but also the undemocratic ethos that resulted from this centralization of power. As the UFW expanded and the task of farmworker advocacy became more complex, the organization should have developed an organizational structure to allow it the flexibility to pursue its goals of social justice in the fields as well as in the legal-political arena. It did not.

After 1981 the union's internal struggles were over. Chavez and followers loyal to him emerged in firm control of the organization.

Those who remained on the executive board and in important positions of power were close family members and friends who had not opposed Chavez during the tumultuous period of restructuring. There were still no union locals; nor was it possible for rank-and-file workers to be voted into positions of leadership within the union without the blessing of the executive board. The ranch committees, originally conceived as intermediaries between the leadership and the workers, were stripped of their power after the revolt by the Salinas representatives. In time, these organizational characteristics would significantly impede the UFW's ability to effectively organize farmworkers, particularly in the central Coast region. During the 1980s, the union shifted its activities to direct mailing and boycott organizing; its organizing in the fields was sharply curtailed. It was this purging and consolidation that allowed Arturo Rodriguez to build the UFW in size and influence during the 1990s. Unfortunately, this retrenchment also facilitated the top-down approach employed in the strawberry campaign that failed to account for micro-level dynamics in the fields.

A New UFW under Rodriguez

By the time of Chavez's death in 1993, the UFW had almost completely stopped organizing in the fields.[5] It had only a handful of contracts covering about 5,000 workers (Mooney and Majka 1995). In the Salinas Valley, a hotbed of union activity in the 1970s, the UFW had just one contract. Most of the contracts held by the union were with small nurseries, mushroom farms, and farms producing other specialty crops, not with extensive row crop operations, as in the past. The ascendancy of Arturo Rodriguez to the helm of the UFW upon Chavez's death opened a new era for the union. Rodriguez began a campaign titled "Every Worker Is an Organizer," signaling a return to the fields. A series of small organizing victories in the mid-1990s led observers to believe that the UFW would once again return to a prominent place as a workers' union in the agriculture industry. By the 1997 march through Watsonville, the UFW was ready for a fight reminiscent of the struggles against the grape and lettuce industries that it had previously organized. However, the UFW of the late 1990s was a very different organization from that of the 1970s and 1980s. It had become a professional political advocacy organization with limited presence in the fields. This shift has had a deleterious effect on the largely immigrant population that the UFW serves.

Theda Skocpol (2003) makes an argument in *Diminished Democracy* that helps explain the consequences of the UFW retreat from the fields. She argues, as others do, that organizations mediate civic participation. They function as schools where members develop the skills necessary to be good citizens. Not only do members learn about issues affecting their communities; they also gain skills in leadership, collective action, and public advocacy. Participation in civic organizations also builds social capital as members expand their networks beyond work and family (Putnam 2000). For these reasons, civic participation via organizations is generally considered good for the democratic health of a society.

Skocpol argues, however, that the emergence during the 1960s of a myriad of advocacy and nonprofit organizations has actually undermined the civic participation of individual members, leading to diminished democracy. These new organizations are professionally managed, and they advocate for, rather than work with, individual members. Skocpol cites a number of reasons for this, but two are significant here. First, government agencies and public policy expansion led to the development of organizations structured in a way that enables them to best effect change within the new institutional frameworks. Second, there is an increased reliance on professional managers to staff these new, sophisticated organizations.[6]

These new organizations are not equipped to foster meaningful civic participation. Members are reduced to names on mailing lists of people who receive newsletters and yearly solicitations for donations, perhaps in exchange for a calendar. Participation has become passive. Professionally administered organizations manage the interests of members in narrow and instrumental ways, with limited participation from the actual rank and file. Skocpol argues that this passivity has significant implications for democratic life in the United States. In my view the deleterious consequences for democratic life of this organized passivity are compounded by the increasing heterogeneity of the nation.

The type of socialization that civic organizations including the UFW have offered in the past is particularly important for immigrant groups. Participation in this type of group connects individuals to their local communities and the political life of the host society. The development of social capital that comes from civic participation facilitates social and cultural integration. These are pro-social processes that are good for immigrants and their host society alike. The fact that the UFW does not function in this capacity has not stopped the union from engendering positive social change on behalf of Latino immigrants in the United States. If the union does not do more for immigrants, however, it risks engaging in a sort of liberal *noblesse oblige* as the self-appointed voice of immigrant farmworkers, and it risks becoming an organization associated with farmworkers in name only. Many farmworkers and other concerned people already believe this to be the case.

The union's identity and behavior are a perennial theme of discussion and debate among well-positioned observers. Philip L. Martin, a labor economist at the University of California–Davis who has spent decades studying the California agriculture industry, encapsulates the issue when he states, "Is it a labor union or a social movement?" Not surprisingly, opinions on the matter vary. Rob Roy, an officer in the Ventura County Growers Association in the southern Central Coast region of California and a vocal critic of the UFW, writes, "Here they are portraying themselves as the voice of California farm workers, and yet they represent less than 1 percent [of the state's farmworkers]" (Alvarez 2002). James Bogart, president of the Grower-Shipper Association of Central California, echoes his colleague's statement when he says, "I don't see any harm in the [union's concentration on social and political work], but they shouldn't go around holding themselves up as a labor organization if their focus is elsewhere" (Alvarez 2002).

Eliseo Medina does not see the emphasis on social and political work as a problem. A former member of the UFW executive board, Medina is currently the international vice president of the Service Employees International Union (SEIU), one of the most dynamic and innovative unions in the US today. According to him, the social movement activities of the union are not a distraction. He claims, "It's very complementary. Where you might get into trouble is where you lose focus of what you're trying to do, which is build power for your members, whether that's in the community, at the ballot box, or in the workplace" (Calvo 2000). Labor economist Martin pushes the tension further when he says that the UFW has had difficulty over the years achieving "a balance between things like negotiating contracts, operating a pension and health care plan, and being sort of a symbol of achievement for Latinos in California" (Calvo 2000).

The UFW's history shows that it is most effective in bringing about social and political change when it works within legal and political institutional arenas. Its strength as a traditional labor union in the agriculture industry is modest. However, the UFW is profoundly invested in its distinctive position as an agriculturally based Mexican-origin labor organization. This identity resonates deeply with many Mexican Americans in the United States who have personal and family experiences in farm labor. The UFW's position as a farm labor–based organization situates it within the history of peasant land struggles surrounding the Mexican Revolution. The similarities between the social justice work of Emiliano Zapata, the Mexican peasant revolutionary, and that of the UFW is often expressed in the union's iconography. Its farm labor roots give the UFW much of its legitimacy as an organization. The strawberry campaign was intended in part to reassert the UFW's dominance as a grassroots-driven farm labor union and initiate a new era of organizing for the AFL-CIO. Determined to breathe life into a faltering labor movement, newly appointed AFL-CIO president John Sweeney looked to the more progressive unions in the AFL-CIO when he took office in 1995. As president of the SEIU, Sweeney presided over some of the most impressive labor victories in the country during the 1980s and 1990s. The success of the SEIU and other unions is due in part to the fact that these unions organized outside the industrial sectors traditionally covered by unions and looked to the nontraditional labor force, including women, immigrants, and other minorities. When the UFW launched the strawberry campaign in 1996, it did so with the enthusiastic support of the AFL-CIO. For the federation, the campaign was to be a continuation of the successful push to increase union membership, particularly among nonwhite, semi-skilled laborers in California. This goal was particularly important for the future of the labor movement in the state, given the increasing proportion of immigrant and minority workers in the state's labor force. Organizing close to 20,000 immigrant workers in an important sector of California's economy would increase the proportion of organized workers in the state and strengthen the position of organized labor in California. For any union, this campaign would have carried special significance, but the UFW is not like other unions. Since its founding it has occupied a unique position as an American social movement.

Looking Ahead: Political Action, Fieldwork, or Both?

Under the charismatic leadership of Cesar Chavez, the UFW became the voice of marginalized America and a symbol of the social and political emergence of people of Mexican descent in mainstream American society. The union's activities during the 1960s and 1970s have also been influential in the evolution of the American labor movement as a whole (Shaw 2008).[7] The UFW's prominence within the American labor movement can be seen in the introduction of certain tactics and strategies, including an emphasis on ethnic labor mobilization and the effective use of institutional mechanisms for social change. These innovations have distinguished the UFW as an organization able to gain major concessions from a powerful industry as well as from the state, and one that has influenced the strategy and structure of the American labor movement. The organization clearly has major significance for those who care about progressive social change in the United States. At the same time, it should not be forgotten that the UFW has been at the spiritual and cultural center of the transition of the Mexican-descent community into mainstream American society. This has changed in the union's recent history. The UFW's current organizational structure limits its integrative potential for current and future immigrant generations. An objective and critical analysis of its 1995–2003 strawberry campaign helps us understand why this is so.

A central and key fact of the strawberry unionization campaign is that the UFW came to Coastal Berry not at the request of workers at the company but rather in response to a strategic decision made by the union leadership. UFW officials, in conjunction with national labor and political leaders, determined that it would be possible to transfer ownership of Coastal Berry, the largest berry producer in the region, to union-friendly investors. The success of these machinations clearly demonstrates the organizational sophistication and institutional capabilities of the UFW. The company's workforce, however, included many workers indifferent, hostile, or estranged from the union. When the union tried to organize workers, it was confronted by powerful social networks. These informal, indigenous organizational structures had a much greater impact on decision making among farmworkers than did UFW organizers. It must be noted, however, that patron-client relations within immigrant social networks are powerful but not insurmountable impediments to unionization. Héctor Delgado (1993) and others have demonstrated that successful labor mobilization can occur among undocumented immigrants who share strong social ties. The problem for the UFW was that after a long absence from the fields, the union's top-down, nondemocratic structure severely limited its abilities to make inroads among the workers at Coastal Berry.

For a majority of workers at Coastal Berry, their subjective assessments toward mobilization were influenced by their social networks to favor not the UFW but their fellow workers: the Comité. It has already been commented that in the long run, the inchoate workers' organization could not have competed against the more robust UFW. Viewing both organizations through the lens of organizational capacity and institutional awareness, however, it is remarkable to that Comité sustained itself for as long as it did—and complicated the UFW's efforts to the extent that it did. The lens of organizational capacity and institutional awareness makes it unremarkable that the UFW was eventually able to secure a contract at the company. The contract the UFW eventually won at Coastal Berry came about as a result of the union's procedural maneuvering within an established institutional arena, not because of its grassroots efforts among rank-and-file workers.

For reform-minded Americans interested in social justice and the welfare of the country's working classes, critically assessing an organization that has championed their cause is not easy. However, to gloss over or ignore the factors that contributed to the UFW's grassroots failure is to commit a disservice to the working poor for the sake of a comforting perception. It is not enough to assert that anti-union growers thwarted the union. Similarly, one cannot simply point at power-hungry supervisors and managers. One-dimensional explanations of the failure of the campaign deny the complexity of social settings. Such accounts most often focus on conditions external to the union, but by focusing on the role of anti-union forces, these approaches shield the union from critical perspectives that could help it grow and become more effective as an advocate for its constituents. At the current juncture, neither the UFW nor the labor movement as a whole can afford to shy away from such scrutiny.

During the strawberry campaign serious efforts were under way to reinvigorate the American labor movement. Responding to dwindling numbers and influence, labor leaders around the country were struggling to identify ways in which unions could thrive and continue to be vital, corrective forces in society. An article published by Rachel Sherman and Kim Voss (2002) during the campaign describes the ways in which certain unions have revitalized the American labor movement. The authors were primarily interested in processes that reversed bureaucratic conservatism. Political crisis within a local union, the introduction of newcomers into it, and increasing pressure from the international union revitalize union locals when all three conditions are met. Before these factors can precipitate change, however, labor organizations must overcome internal resistance to change. Doing so has not been easy for many unions.

Sherman and Voss have studied varying degrees of innovation within the SEIU and Hotel Employees and Restaurant Employees Union (HERE) locals to explain their hypotheses regarding union revitalization. These two unions often gain attention for their dynamism and growth. Their success in the face of a starkly adverse climate for labor organization is the result of serious and often difficult self-reflection. A profile on Andy Stern, president of the SEIU, in the *New York Times Magazine* illustrates the struggle that this self-referential analysis has created within the movement (Bai 2005). Stern changed the organizational culture and structure of the SEIU and in the process made it more effective. He then planned to radically alter the AFL-CIO to make it more aggressive and responsive to the needs of workers.

Stern's agenda was not without its detractors within organized labor. Five years after the piece was written, Stern stepped down from his position as head of the SEIU. It is not within the scope of this study to render judgment on Stern's vision for the AFL-CIO. The point rather is to note that Stern has been willing to look inward and initiate frank dialogue about the future of the movement. Too often, it seems union leaders have abdicated responsibility for the decline of labor, choosing instead to look outside their organizations for blame and answers. If the UFW is to continue in its position as a vanguard organization within the American labor movement, it would do well to heed Stern's example and look within itself to find ways to be more effective and responsive to its core constituents. This work will not only strengthen the union and the labor movement; it will also strengthen American democracy by helping to incorporate immigrants into the union and into American society.

Scholars of collective action in modern societies remind us that it is imprudent to conceive of social movements without also invoking notions of participatory democracy. Charles Tilly argues, "The rise of [national social movements] belongs to the same complex of changes which included two other profound transformations in the character of popular collective action—the growth of national electoral politics, and the proliferation of created associations as vehicles of action" (in Bright and Harding 1984: 304). Tarrow expands on this point when he defines social movements as "collective challenges by people with common purposes and solidarity in sustained interaction with elites, opponents, and authorities" (1994: 3-4). Both theorists emphasize the dynamic matrix of democracy in which collective action for social change occurs.

In California and the rest of the United States, labor can be used successfully as a vehicle for social and political change and for immigrant incorporation. As an organization that identifies with the largest ethnic groups in the state, the UFW has the opportunity to make a positive impact on the lives of immigrants. If this potential is to be realized, however, the UFW must understand that its oligarchic leadership, lack of meaningful grassroots participation, and its nearly exclusive dependence on institutional strategies have led to its failure to have greater relevance for the lives of farmworkers. Should the union direct its organizational prowess at the state's farmworkers as well as the state's institutions, it might cultivate an active membership as well as a civically engaged class of farmworkers who might further propel political change that supports labor organizing. Difficult as it may be, an honest evaluation will provide a better understanding of the complex relationship between organized labor and disenfranchised workers. As an attempt to provide this type of analysis, this book hopes to serve the interests of working people and their advocates.

---

[1] The argument for unionization is further weakened when one considers that Coastal Berry's wages and benefits were already among the best in the industry. Workers at the company did not work under the exploitive conditions experienced by workers at smaller, more marginal operations.

[2] The astute reader may at this point recall that support for the Comité among workers was based, in part, on their relative job satisfaction and their aversion to UFW tactics. One might argue that because of the nature of this support, it does not necessarily follow that the Comité was promoting immigrant empowerment and social incorporation. Furthermore, given the self-interested use of patron-client ties by some in the Comité leadership, the reader may find my argument to be naïve or ideal. The claim is certainly ideal, but it is not naïve. Groups like the Comité, when fully formed and articulated, serve the interests of immigrants and civil society. Because the inchoate Comité did not function in this way does not mean that it could not eventually do so. When it ceased to exist, the possibility that the group could function as a vehicle for immigrant empowerment and social incorporation was also extinguished.

[3] More detailed and thorough description of these events can be found in Bardacke (2011) and Pawel (2009).

[4] Majka (1981) also recounts the events surrounding the dismissal of the Salinas workers.

[5] Many observers will cite internal organizational strife and a changing political environment to explain the UFW's retreat from the fields in the 1980s (e.g., Majka and Majka 1995; Pawel 2009). Martin (2003) argues that employer restructuring and immigration may be more important factors that inhibit farm labor mobilization. He notes that the unanticipated but significant increase in farm labor contractors and custom harvesters as intermediary employers made organizing very difficult. Furthermore, sustained immigration from Mexico and short "careers" in farmwork further exacerbated an already inauspicious organizing environment. The strawberry industry did not experience the same rise in intermediary employers during this time period as did other sectors of the California agriculture industry. However, the number of very small-scale, poorly financed producers (usually former workers) did expand, and this process was also not conducive to farm labor mobilization.

[6] Staggenborg (1991) makes a similar argument about the emergence of social movement professionals and the implications of their presence in the structure of social movement organizations.

[7] A striking observation from my research is the unusually high number of people in the labor movement who at some point were affiliated with the UFW. This strong association suggests a broad diffusion of personnel as well as ideas from the UFW to other groups committed to the idea of social justice. My observations are consistent with those of Shaw (2008), who argues that the UFW has significantly influenced a broad range of contemporary progressive social movements in the United States.

Appendix A
A Note on Methodology

Studying the Comité and the UFW did not prove easy. I arrived in Watsonville without really knowing anyone directly associated with the strawberry campaign. Although the campaign had technically been over for some time when I arrived, it was still a sensitive issue. Many workers as well as company personnel were waiting for tensions to relax so that the situation in the fields could normalize. I sensed that few people were excited to relive the events of the campaign in interviews with an outsider asking questions about what had taken place. Still, I persisted. Over the course of my time in Watsonville I was able to conduct fifty-three in-depth interviews conducted with strawberry pickers, campaign organizers, union leaders, industry officials, Coastal Berry personnel, local farmers, and community leaders. Discussing the campaign with a wide range of individuals directly and indirectly related to the campaign enabled me to develop an understanding of the events from multiple frames of reference.

I began my investigation by making formal inquiries with the Coastal Berry Company. Earnie Farley, the recently promoted president, was open and provided good information, yet he was apprehensive about letting me speak directly to workers in the fields. An uneasy calm had descended in the fields, and Farley did not want to reignite old tensions. Still, he put me in contact with other individuals with the company. Through Earnie Farley, I was able to access workers at different levels of the company hierarchy, including members of the professional staff, supervisors, and crew foremen. Farley also introduced me to Sergio Leal, an early leader of the Comité; at the time of the interviews, he was the organization's president. Leal proved willing to speak with me and eagerly connected me with other supporters of the Comité. It was also through Sergio Leal that I was able to communicate with Comité employees and legal counsels.

Finding UFW supporters proved to be a bit more difficult. I found many of the long-time UFW officials wary of my requests for interviews. Despite repeated written communication I was unable to interview Arturo Rodriguez. I was, however, able to have several telephone conversations with Marc Grossman, long-time UFW spokesperson. He was knowledgeable and engaging in these conversations, but I also recognized that as a public relations professional, he was very cognizant of what information he was providing as well as the way in which the information was framed. I had more luck accessing information on the UFW from recently hired personnel or personnel no longer affiliated with the union. This included organizers as well as other professional staff who were more open about their experiences and thoughts on the campaign. These UFW-affiliated personnel connected me with pro-UFW workers in the fields. I was also able to access pro-UFW workers through local reporters who were familiar with the case and knew workers on both sides of the conflict. In the end I was able to access a roughly equal number of workers who were for the Comité or for the UFW. It is important to note, however, that many of the workers—even those who professed loyalty to one side or the other—were agnostic about the whole issue. About a third were strong UFW supporters, a third strong Comité supporters, and a third lacked strong inclinations one way or the other.

In addition to workers and company personnel, I felt it was important to learn about the community and the industry in which the campaign occurred. I once again found local reporters to be very helpful. Not only did they possess a wealth of information, they were also able to put me in contact with a wide range of individuals directly or indirectly connected to the campaign. With the help of reporters I was able to interview a number of farmers—many who were strawberry farmers—in the Pajaro Valley. These farmers provided valuable information in their views with respect to farming and worker-grower relations. The interviews were also useful in getting a historical context for the relationship between the UFW and farming community. To get to know the industry better, I contacted marketing and public relations personnel at the large strawberry cooperatives as well as the California Strawberry Alliance, headquartered in Watsonville. From these interviews I was able to acquire background information on the industry as well as the industry perspective on the campaign. In addition to interviews with farmers and strawberry industry professionals, I sought out interviews with officials from other unions in the area. These union leaders had been close observers of the campaign, even if they themselves were not directly involved. I found their impressions to be especially interesting.

They were clearly pro-labor, but they were not necessarily pro-UFW. They were, however, insightful and nuanced in their views of the grower-worker relations in the industry.

If there was one commonality among these three disparate groups—farmers, industry, and union officials—it was that they did not fall into conventional stereotypes. I met one farmer with an MBA who praised the relationship he had with a union. A union official praised farmers in the local area for the working conditions and benefits they offered. All were willing participants, keen to answer my questions in order to help me understand the events surrounding the strawberry campaign.

As mentioned earlier, not everyone was eager to speak with me. This was not only on the part of the UFW. One of the first farmers I contacted was hostile due to my Yale University affiliation because an undergraduate group at Yale had sent local farmers a letter in support of farmworkers, which many in the farmer community took to be uninformed and condescending. An anti-union consultant who had very recently been extremely active in anti-UFW work claimed that terminal illness prevented any possible communication whatsoever. And finally, many workers were themselves wary of speaking with an outsider whom they did not know. This reticence is understandable among a population that included many undocumented workers in a context of rampant anti-immigration. I would go on to find that miscommunication was rife and that rumor and innuendo easily substituted for truth among farmworkers who had limited access to outside sources of knowledge. Even when I did manage to interview workers I found them to be cautious and guarded. Since many workers were from the Mexican state Michoacán, I would point out that my family hailed from this region as well. I started to do this in the hope of eliciting some sort of feeling of communication. This was rarely the case. It didn't matter that we shared a geographical connection. As an academic, my place on the Central Coast was very different from theirs.

In addition to the interviews, I reviewed a great deal of documentary evidence related to the campaign. I examined newspaper accounts, industry and union publications such as newsletters, court records, and other government documents. The campaign took a litigious turn, and this proved a boon to me. There were hundreds of pages of documents from the California Agriculture Labor Relations Board (ALRB), including formal hearings, findings, rulings, and affidavits. All were rich sources of data that helped round out my understanding of what had taken place. I also reviewed dozens of articles written in the local, regional, and national press related to the campaign. These articles not only provided a sense of the campaign in the workers' own words but also allowed me to determine the overall trajectory of events. I found industry and union newsletters to be valuable sources, too. These publications weren't preoccupied with objectivity, and because of this they provided an unfettered perspective on the position and interests of these two opposing groups. Industry publications, for example, would provide instructions on dealing with the possibility of a unionization campaign. The UFW newsletter tended to focus on recent achievements, which seemed intended to keep up morale.

Every piece of data, regardless of source, contained some explicit or implicit bias. This was more obvious in some cases than others—for example, a UFW newsletter or an industry publication. However, even more purportedly neutral sources such as an ALRB report contained some implied bias. Here, the bias would be the result of the intended aims or objective of the report. This would result in the inclusion of some material and, more important, the exclusion of other material. This is not a claim about ulterior motives on the part of the ALRB or any other organization or individual. The point simply is that whatever is not said, or written, is often just as important as that which has been presented. My task as a researcher, then, was to take these various pieces of data and cross-examine their presentation of events. This form of data triangulation would allow me to "explain more fully, the richness and complexity of human behavior by studying it from more than one standpoint" (Cohen and Manion 1986: 254). So, for example, in assessing some particular instance of unrest, I would review interview material from pro-UFW workers, pro-Comité workers, neutral workers, and company personnel. I would then cross-reference these findings with data available from the ALRB and newspaper records.

While it would be imprudent for a researcher to make claims about absolute objectivity in the rendering of events, it is possible to obtain a fuller, more rich understanding by taking into account multiple and possibly competing perspectives on the same phenomenon. I believe I was able to achieve this in my review of the relevant material. This allowed me to arrive at a fair and accurate assessment of the events related to the unionization campaign in the Central Coast strawberry industry.

Appendix B

A Timeline of Events: The UFW and Coastal Berry 1993–2004

1993

April 23: UFW President Cesar Chavez dies. A few months later his son-in-law Arturo Rodriguez assumes leadership of the organization.

1994

March: The UFW retraces its historic 1966 march from Delano, California, to Sacramento. Leadership decides to return to the fields.

1995

August: Workers at VCNM Farms in Salinas organize and carry out an unauthorized wildcat strike. Company owners eventually plow the crop under rather than respect workers' wishes to unionize.

1996

February: Under the leadership of Rodriguez, the UFW has now won thirteen elections, and its membership has increased by 4,000.

November: John Sweeney, recently elected president of the AFL-CIO, launches the National Strawberry Commission for Workers Rights to coordinate the strawberry campaign nationwide and forge coalitions with various civic, environmental, and religious groups. The UFW releases a report titled "Five Cents for Fairness: The Case for Change in the Strawberry Fields."

December: The Strawberry Workers and Farmers Alliance, a pro-industry group from Ventura County, accuses the UFW of misleading the public with its Five Cents for Fairness campaign.

1997

January 30: Sergio Soto, an anti-labor specialist involved with the Pro-Workers Committee in Watsonville, also involved in creating the, makes a presentation at the board of directors meeting of the Western Growers Association. The UFW will later obtain minutes of the meeting and use them as evidence of a relationship between growers' groups and anti-union workers' groups.

April 13: The UFW leads between 17,000 and 30,000 people in a march through the streets of Watsonville in support of workers' rights to organize. The march signals the beginning of the campaign to organize 20,000 workers in the California strawberry industry.

April 29: Seven religious leaders and actor Martin Sheen are arrested while protesting outside the Gargiulo Farms offices in Watsonville.

May: The UFW files thirty-three notices to take access and twenty-one notices to organize among various farms in the Central Coast region.

May 30: American Stores Company, owner of the Lucky grocery chain, announces that it will "endorse the rights of strawberry pickers to organize and bargain collectively."

June 2: The UFW files a petition to gain access to fields at Gargiulo Company.

June 17: Gargiulo is sold to investors David Gladstone and Landon Butler. The new owners pledge neutrality in the unionization drive. The company is renamed the Coastal Berry Company.

June 27: Gargiulo agrees to pay $575,000 in back wages to hundreds of workers forced to work before going on the clock.

August 8: With the help of the UFW, three raspberry pickers file a class-action suit on behalf of hundreds of workers against Reiter Berry Farms for not paying workers required overtime pay. The suit demands back pay to 1993 for 360 pickers at a total cost of $750,000.

August 10: An estimated 3,500 workers march through Watsonville denouncing the UFW organizing campaign. The UFW accuses one of the lead organizations, the Agricultural Workers Committee (AWC), of being a "front group" for four strawberry growers. The UFW subsequently files suits against the growers with the ALRB, arguing that growers Ed Kelly, Clint Miller, Miguel Ramos, and Jim Dutra encouraged and coerced workers to attend the march.

August 12: Company officials of the Ralphs supermarket chain in Southern California meet with Coastal Berry Company personnel to express support for Coastal Berry's position of neutrality toward the UFW's unionization efforts.

August 20: The UFW holds a rally outside Driscoll Strawberry Associates demanding that the company honor its public statements regarding its position of neutrality toward worker unionization.

September 16: Safeway, the second-largest food retailer in the country, agrees to honor workers' rights to organize.

October 14: The UFW files a lawsuit in the Superior Court of California in Santa Cruz arguing that growers and growers' groups have supported anti-UFW groups.

November 14: The UFW calls for labor and consumer support in Connecticut and attempts to have supermarkets sign pledges of support for strawberry unionization efforts.

December: Landon Butler sells his half of the Coastal Berry Company to David Gladstone, making Gladstone sole owner of the company.

1998
January: David Smith is hired as president of the Coastal Berry Company.

January 3: The UFW files a second lawsuit against the AWC, seeking attorney fees after the AWC tried unsuccessfully to block the initial suit against the anti-UFW group.

January 26: A judge rules that the UFW lawsuit can move forward; the union is awarded $8,000 in legal fees.

March 19: Folk music group Peter, Paul, and Mary perform a benefit concert for the UFW in Santa Cruz.

March 28: More than 1,000 people march in New York City in solidarity with the UFW. Feminist Gloria Steinem speaks at the event.

May 6: The Ventura County Agricultural Association files an unfair labor practice petition with the ALRB, charging that the UFW is threatening, coercing, and harassing Coastal Berry workers. Coastal Berry and the union deny the charges.

June 16: The city council of Salinas passes a resolution recognizing the rights of workers to organize. Months earlier, the city of Santa Cruz had passed a similar resolution.

June 17: The Western Growers Association files a lawsuit in the Superior Court of California in Santa Cruz against the UFW and Coastal Berry for illegally conspiring to unionize workers. The plaintiffs contend that Coastal Berry is engaging in unfair labor practices by publicly stating its neutrality while sending letters to workers expressing its support of the union. In the suit the WGA also alleges that Gargiulo was never actually sold by Monsanto.

July 1: A demonstration staged by anti-UFW workers turns violent when an estimated 150 anti-UFW pickers attack 75 pro-UFW pickers at Coastal Berry's fruit cooling facility in Watsonville. Several people are injured; one man, Jose Guadalupe Fernández, is arrested.

July 18: The Coastal Berry Farm Workers Committee (El Comité) files a petition for election with the Salinas office of the ALRB. According to the California Agricultural Labor Relations Act (ALRA), the election must take place within seven days of the petition's submission. The UFW files unfair labor practice (ULP) objections with the ALRB against the Comité and Coastal Berry.

July 21: A California Labor Federation meeting is held in Oakland. Senator Barbara Boxer and Democratic gubernatorial candidate Gray Davis are in attendance. Rodriguez accuses Coastal Berry of promoting terrorism and declares the Comité to be a sham. Legislators in Sacramento lobby in favor of the union, and the UFW holds a rally at ALRB offices in Salinas and Sacramento asking that the Coastal Berry election be blocked.

July 23: Despite numerous objections from the UFW, the Coastal Berry election is held. Calling the election "a farce and a mockery," the UFW abstains from participation. Workers at the company will choose between the Comité and "none" as their representative.

July 24: Hundreds of Coastal Berry workers walk off their jobs to protest the election. Coastal Berry accuses the UFW of masterminding the walk-out, which the UFW claims is a spontaneous worker action. Election results are released. The Comité wins the election with 523 votes in its favor compared to 410 votes against.

July 25: Coastal Berry files a civil suit against the UFW seeking damages incurred by worker walk-outs. The company president says workers who do not return to their jobs will be replaced.

July 29: The ALRB draws sharp criticism from labor leaders and lawmakers for allowing the election to take place despite claims that the Comité is a sham and that it has engaged in violence and intimidation. The ALRB defends its decision.

July 31: The UFW claims in a press release that the Comité failed to notify 162 workers in Ventura County about the election. If so, nearly 15 percent of Coastal Berry's 1,200 employees were not given the opportunity to vote.

August 5: The ALRB decides that more time is needed before the July 23 election results can be certified because the UFW has raised "novel legal issues" that require more attention. Certification is deferred until at least August 21.

August 7: Coastal Berry owner David Gladstone files objections to the election. Similar to those of the UFW, the objections state that the Comité created an atmosphere of fear and intimidation. The UFW maintains that the Comité is a company union despite Gladstone's objections.

September 14: The UFW protests outside ALRB offices in Salinas claiming that the labor board is dragging its feet in the investigation of objections to the election.

November 5: Judge Thomas Sobel issues a preliminary decision voiding the Coastal Berry election because 162 workers in Ventura County were not given the opportunity to vote. The Comité has until November 18 to appeal the decision.

November 9: The UFW produces bank records to support its contention that agribusiness supported anti-union efforts. According to bank statements, the Pro Workers Committee and other groups that grew out of this organization received more than $56,000 in donations from growers and other agricultural interests. Among the companies and organizations implicated in wrongdoing are New West Fruit Corp., Del Llano Farms, Saticoy Berry Farms in Oxnard, Watsonville Berry Cooler, Premier Growers Association, Clint Miller Farms, and the Western Growers Association.

November 19: Governor-elect Gray Davis names Arturo Rodriguez to an "elite panel" charged with developing policy recommendations for water usage and other agricultural matters.

December 21: Reiter Berry Farms agrees to pay almost 500 berry pickers $283,000 for work without pay before and after shifts during the 1994–1997 seasons. Reiter Berry Farms is one of the largest suppliers of berries to Driscoll Associates.

1999
January 7: Growers voice the concern that their political power may erode with the election of Gray Davis as governor. Davis's three new appointments to the ALRB are cited as evidence that the power of the UFW may be bolstered by his administration.

February: Earnie Farley becomes president of the Coastal Berry Company.

May 20: About eighteen strawberry growers and farm groups agree to stop funding workers' committees that rival the UFW. The UFW claims that workers' committees are committing fraud by claiming to be independent when they are actually funded by growers.

May 28: The UFW fails to win a second election at the Coastal Berry Company. Vote counts are 577 in favor of the Comité and 646 in favor of UFW; 79 workers vote for no union at all. The UFW notes that 60 ballots are unresolved. The election results are seen as a stunning blow to the UFW.

June 2: Most undecided ballots go to the Comité. The final vote is 670 in favor of the Comité, 589 in favor of the UFW, and 83 workers voting for no union. Since neither union receives a majority 682 votes, a runoff election is to be held without a "no union" option.

June 3 and 4: Runoff election results are 688 in favor of the Comité to 598 in favor of the UFW. An outcome-determining 92 ballots are disputed.

July 7: Seven hundred fifty workers at Basic Vegetables in King City, in the southern Salinas Valley, go on strike.

August 17: The Comité is declared winner in the Coastal Berry election. Final election results are 725 workers for the Comité and 616 workers for UFW. The UFW files more than 200 objections against the election.

October 14: ALRB executive secretary Antonio Barboza orders a hearing for December 7 in Salinas to investigate the UFW's objections to the Coastal Berry election. Barboza issues a report contending that nearly half of the UFW's 234 objections to the election warrant further review; he asserts, however, that the UFW must prove the charges of misconduct. Jim Gumberg, attorney for the Comité, accuses the UFW of dragging out the whole election process. Of the 234 objections to the election, the ALRB decides to send 100 to an administrative law judge. The UFW appeals the decision to set aside the remaining 134 objections.

2000
March 7: Judge Thomas Sobel decides that workers in Ventura County can be represented by the UFW while workers in Watsonville should be represented by the Comité. The vote in the Ventura County runoff election had been 321 in favor of the UFW to 277 in favor of the Comité.

2002
November: An election is held at Coastal Berry to decertify the Comité as the workers' bargaining agent. Workers side with the UFW against the Comité.

2003
June: The UFW signs a contract with the Coastal Berry Company. The union will be the sole bargaining agent covering all workers in the company's Northern and Southern California operations.

2004

October: The Coastal Berry Company is sold to the Dole Food Company.

Bibliography

Agricultural Labor Relations Board. 1999a. *Case No. 99-RC-4-SAL*, October 14.
———. 1999b. *Decision of Administrative Law Judge*, December 7.
Alvarez, Fred. 1999a. "Area growers fear power may erode under Davis." *Los Angeles Times*, January 7.
———. 1999b. "Coastal Berry tops UFW in balloting." *Los Angeles Times*, August 18.
———. 2002. "Dispute over size of UFW is reopened." *Los Angeles Times*, June 10.
Associated Press. 1998. "Strawberry workers walk out." *Bakersfield Californian*, July 24.
Bacon, David. 1996. "Putting L.A. on the Map." *Village Voice*, March 19.
———. 1997. "The UFW picks strawberries." *Nation*, 264:14.
———. 1998. "Strawberry jam: Grower ploy dash UFW dreams in strawberry fields." *LA Weekly*, September 17.
———. 1998. "A company union battles the UFW in Watsonville." http://dbacon.igc.org/FarmWork/01coast.html. Retrieved October 10, 1998.
Bai, Matt. 2005. "The New Boss." *New York Times*, January 30.
Baldwin Hick, Virginia, and Robert Steyer. 1997. "Monsanto sells strawberry farms: Buyer agrees to stay neutral in union voting." *St. Louis Post Dispatch*, June 18.
Bardacke, Frank. 1993. "The decline and fall of the UFW." *Nation*, July 26/August 2.
———. 1997. "After the marchers go home." *Nation*, April 7.
———. 2002. "Cesar Chavez: The Serpent and the Dove." In C. Davis and D. Igler, eds., *The Human Tradition in California*. Wilmington, DE: Scholarly Resources.
———. 2011. *Trampling Out the Vintage: Cesar Chavez and the Two Souls of the United Farm Workers*. London: Verso.
Barnett, Tracy. 1996. "Fresh campaign." *Santa Cruz County Sentinel*, May 19.
———. 1997. "Driscoll growers say UFW intent is 'rule or ruin.'" *Santa Cruz County Sentinel*, August 21.
Barnett, Tracy, and Maria Garcia. 1996. "Passions run high in the fields." *Santa Cruz County Sentinel*, August 16.
Berger, Peter L. and Thomas Luckmann. 1966. *The Social Construction of Reality: a Treatise in the Sociology of Knowledge*. Garden City, NY: Anchor.

Bourdieu. Pierre. 1977. *Outline of a Theory of Practice.* Cambridge: Cambridge University Press.

———. 1996. *The State Nobility: Elite Schools in the Field of Power.* Stanford, CA: Stanford University Press.

Brazil, Eric. 1998a. "Unions huddle in Oakland." *San Francisco Examiner,* July 21.

———. 1998b. "UFW berry pickers strike after fractious union vote." *San Francisco Examiner,* July 25.

Bronfenbrenner, Kate, and Tom Juravich. 2001. "The Evolution of Strategic and Coordinated Bargaining Campaigns in the 1990s: The Steelworkers' Experience." In L. Turner, H. C. Katz, and R. W. Hurd, eds., *Rekindling the Movement: Labor's Quest for Relevance in the 21st Century.* Ithaca, NY: Cornell University Press.

Browne, William P. 1988. *Private Interests, Public Policy, and American Agriculture.* Lawrence: University Press of Kansas.

Burt, Ronald S. 1997. "The Contingency Value of Social Capital." *Administrative Science Quarterly* 42(2):339–365.

Buttel, Frederick H., Olaf F. Larson, and Gilbert W. Gillespie Jr. *The Sociology of Agriculture.* New York: Greenwood.

Calavita, Kitty. 1992. *Inside the State: The Bracero Program, Immigration, and the INS.* New York: Routledge.

Calvo, Dana. 2000. "UFW toils in new field: Cities." *Los Angeles Times,* May 26.

Chan, Sucheng. 1986. *This Bittersweet Soil: the Chinese in California Agriculture, 1860–1910.* Berkeley: University of California Press.

Chibnik, Michael, ed. 1987. *Farm Work and Field Work: American Agriculture in Anthropological Perspective.* Ithaca, NY: Cornell University Press.

Clark, Karen. 1999. "Davis marks berry dispute with 'stealth' board picks." *Santa Cruz County Sentinel,* January 28.

Cleeland, Nancy. 1999. "When the foreman is dad." *Los Angeles Times,* September 23.

Clemens, Elisabeth S. 1996. "Organizing Form as Frame: Collective Identity and Political Strategy in the American Labor Movement." In D. McAdam, J. D. McCarthy, and M. N. Zald, eds., *Comparative Perspectives of Social Movements: Political Opportunities, Mobilizing Structures, and Cultural Framing.* Cambridge: Cambridge University Press.

———. 1997. *The People's Lobby: Organizational Innovation and the Rise of Interest Group Politics in the United States, 1890-1925.* Chicago: University of Chicago Press.

Cohen, Jerome. 1986. "UFW must get back to organizing." *Los Angeles Times,* January 15.

Cohen, Louis, and Lawrence Manion. 1986. *Research Methods in Education.* London: Croom Helm.

Cornelius, Wayne. 1977. "Leaders, Followers, and Official Patrons in Urban Mexico." In S. W. Schmidt, J. C. Scott, and C. Landé, eds., *Friends, Followers, and Factions: A Reader in Political Clientelism.* Berkeley: University of California Press.

Cranford, Cynthia J. 2005. "Networks of Exploitation: Immigrant Labor and the Restructuring of the Los Angeles Janitorial Industry." *Social Problems* 52(3):379–397.

Daniel, Cletus E. 1981. *Bitter Harvest: A History of California Farmworkers, 1870–1941.* Ithaca, NY: Cornell University Press.

DeBare, Ilana. 1997. "Safeway signs pact with UFW in support of strawberry workers accord represents big turnaround for former adversaries." *San Francisco Chronicle,* September 16.

Delgado, Héctor L. 1993. *New Immigrants, Old Unions: Organizing Undocumented Workers in Los Angeles.* Philadelphia: Temple University Press.

DiMaggio, Paul. 1985. "Structural Analysis of Organizational Fields: A Blockmodel Approach." *Research in Organizational Behavior* 8:355–370.

DiMaggio, Paul, and Walter W. Powell. 1983. "The Iron Cage Revisited: Institutional Isomorphism and Collective Rationality in Organizational Fields." *American Sociological Review* 48(2):147–160.

Dobbin, Frank, ed. 2004. *The New Economic Sociology: A Reader.* Princeton, NJ: Princeton University Press.

Dryzek, John S., David Downes, Christian Hunold, David Schlosberg, and Hans-Christian Hernes. 2003. *Green States and Social Movements: Environmentalism in the United States, United Kingdom, Germany, and Norway.* Oxford: Oxford University Press.

Edid, Maralyn. 1994. *Farm Labor Organizing: Trends and Prospects.* Ithaca, NY: ILR Press.

Fisher, Lawrence M. 1995. "Monsanto to acquire 49.9% of biotechnology company." *New York Times,* June 29.

Fligstein, Neil. 2001. *The Architecture of Markets: An Economic Sociology of Capitalist Societies.* Princeton, NJ: Princeton University Press.

Friedland, William H., Amy E. Barton, and Robert J. Thomas. 1981. *Manufacturing Green Gold: Capital, Labor, and Technology in the Lettuce Industry.* New York: Cambridge University Press.

Friedland, William H., Lawrence Busch, Frederick H. Buttel, and Alan Rudy. 1991. *Towards a New Political Economy of Agriculture.* Boulder, CO: Westview.

Friedrich, Paul. 1968. "The Legitimacy of a Cacique." In M. J Swartz, ed., *Local-Level Politics: Social and Cultural Perspectives.* Chicago: Aldine.

———. 1977. *Agrarian Revolt in a Mexican Village.* Chicago: University of Chicago Press.

García, Mario T. 1989. *Mexican Americans: Leadership, Ideology, Identity, 1930–1960.* New Haven, CT: Yale University Press.

Ganz, Marshall. 2000. "Resources and Resourcefulness: Strategic Capacity in the Unionization of California Agriculture, 1959–1966." *American Journal of Sociology* 105(4):1003–1062.

———. 2009. *Why David Sometimes Wins: Leadership, Organization, and Strategy in the California Farm Worker Movement.* New York: Oxford University Press.

Gaura, Maria Alicia. 1998a. "Rivals of UFW win right to berry vote: Union absent from today's election." *San Francisco Chronicle,* July 23.

———. 1998b. "Strawberry workers rebuff UFW: In-house labor organization to negotiate with growers." *San Francisco Examiner,* July 29.

Geertz, Clifford. 1973. *The Interpretation of Cultures.* New York: Basic.

Gerth, H. H., and C. Wright Mills. 1946. *From Max Weber: Essays in Sociology.* New York: Oxford University Press.

González, Gilbert G. 1999. *Mexican Consuls and Labor Organizing: Imperial Politics in the American Southwest.* Austin: University of Texas Press.

Gonzales, Juan L. 1985. *Mexican and Mexican American Farm Workers: The California Agricultural Industry.* New York: Praeger.

Granovetter, Mark S. 1973. "The Strength of Weak Ties." *American Journal of Sociology* 78(6):1360–1380.

Guerin-Gonzales, Camille. 1994. *Mexican Workers and American Dreams.* New Brunswick, NJ: Rutgers University Press.

Gutiérrez, David G. 1995. *Walls and Mirrors: Mexican Americans, Mexican Immigrants, and the Politics of Ethnicity.* Berkeley: University of California Press.

Hall, Greg. 2001. *Harvest Wobblies: The Industrial Workers of the World and Agricultural Laborers in the American West, 1905–1930.* Corvallis: Oregon State University Press.

Hanley, Christine. 1999. "Labor panel to hear challenges in strawberry union debate." *San Francisco Chronicle*, October 28.

Hansen, John Mark. 1991. *Gaining Access: Congress and the Farm Lobby, 1919-1981.* Chicago: University of Chicago Press.

Hansen, Roger D. 1971. *The Politics of Mexican Development.* Baltimore: Johns Hopkins University Press.

Hawley, Amos. 1968. "Human Ecology." In D. L. Sills, ed., *International Encyclopedia of the Social Science.* New York: Macmillan.

Hays, Sharon. 1994. "Structure and Agency and the Sticky Problem of Culture." *Sociological Theory* 12(1):57–72.

Heilbroner, Robert L. 1986. *The Essential Adam Smith.* New York: W.W. Norton.

Henneman, Todd. 1998. "Judge quashes workers' vote for strawberry union: 162 employees missed in election." *San Francisco Chronicle*, November 10.

Henshaw, Jake. 1998. "Lawmakers, UFW fighting union election." *San Jose Mercury News*, July 22.

Jenkins, J. Craig, and Charles Perrow. 1977. "Insurgency of the Powerless: Farm Worker Movements (1946–1972)." *American Sociological Review* 42:249–268.

Johnston, Paul. 2004. "Outflanking Power, Reframing Unionism: The Basic Strike of 1999–2001." *Labor Studies Journal* 28(4):1–24.

Kleist, Trina. 1999. "Union tug-of-war enmeshed local strawberry workers." *Santa Cruz County Sentinel*, November 29.

Krissman, Fred. 2005. "Sin Coyote Ni Patrón: Why the 'Migrant Network' Fails to Explain International Migration." *International Migration Review* 39(1):4–44.

Lawrence, Steve. 1998. "Labor leaders, lawmakers blast ALRB's handling of strawberry election." *San Francisco Examiner*, July 29.

Lifsher, Marc. 1998. "How Monsanto and Democrats failed in efforts to aid UFW." *Wall Street Journal*, August 5.

———. 1999a. "ALRB shuffle stalls hearing on union vote." *Wall Street Journal*, January 27.

———. 1999b. "Confidential memo suggests Coastal Berry favored UFW." *Wall Street Journal*, October 13.

Lin, Nan. 1999. "Social Networks and Status Attainment." *Annual Review of Sociology* 25:467–487.

Linneman, Bob. 1997. "Group a 'front' for growers, UFW alleges." *Santa Cruz County Sentinel*, August 9.

London, Joan, and Henry Anderson. 1970. *So Ye Shall Reap: The Story of Cesar Chavez and the Farm Workers' Movement.* New York: Apollo Editions.

Lordan, Betsy. 1996. "UFW opens strawberry industry drive." *Monterey County Herald*, June 1.

Majka, Linda C. 1981. "Labor Militancy among Farm Workers and the Strategy of Protest: 1900–1979." *Social Problems* 28:533–547.

Majka, Theo. 1980. "People's Movements and Farm Labor Insurgency." *Contemporary Crisis* 4:283–308.

Majka, Linda C., and Theo J. Majka. 1982. *Farm Workers, Agribusiness, and the State.* Philadelphia: Temple University Press.

Majka, Theo J., and Linda C. Majka. 1992. "Decline of the Farm Labor Movement in California: Organizational Crisis and Political Change." *Critical Sociology* 19:3–36.

Márquez, Benjamin. 2003. *Constructing Identities in Mexican American Political Organizations.* Austin: University of Texas Press.

Martin, Philip L. 1988. *Harvest of Confusion: Migrant Workers in US Agriculture.* Boulder, CO: Westview.

———. 2003. *Promise Unfulfilled: Unions, Immigration, and the Farm Workers.* Ithaca, NY: Cornell University/ILR Press.

Massey, Douglas S. 1987. "Understanding Mexican Migration to the United States." *American Journal of Sociology* 92:1372–1403.

Massey, Douglas S., and Felipe Garcia España. 1987. "The Social Process of International Migration." *Science* 14:733–738.

Massey, Douglas S., Jorge Durand, and Nolan J. Malone. 2002. *Beyond Smoke and Mirrors: Mexican Immigration in an Era of Economic Integration.* New York: Russell Sage Foundation.

Massey, Douglas S., Luin Goldring, and Jorge Durand. 1994. "Continuity in Transnational Migration: An Analysis of Nineteen Mexican Communities." *American Journal of Sociology* 99:1492–1533.

Massey, Douglas S., Rafael Alarcón, Jorge Durand, and Humberto González. 1987. *Return to Aztlan: The Social Process of International Migration from Western Mexico.* Berkeley: University of California Press.

Maxwell, Lesli A. "Valley man voted into number 2 post." *Fresno Bee*, September 4.

McAdam, Doug. 1982. *Political Process and the Development of Black Insurgency, 1930–1970.* Chicago: University of Chicago Press.

McAdam, Doug, John D. McCarthy, and Mayer N. Zald, eds. 1996. *Comparative Perspectives of Social Movements: Political Opportunities, Mobilizing Structures, and Cultural Framing.* Cambridge: Cambridge University Press.

McCarthy, Charles. 1996. "National speakers stoke labor organizing fires." *Fresno Bee,* September 2.

McCarthy, John D., and Mayer N. Zald. 1977. "Resource Mobilization and Social Movements: A Partial Theory." *American Journal of Sociology* 82:1212–1241.

Merrill, Michael. 1997. "Thousands march against UFW." *Register-Pajaronian*, August 11.

———. 1998a. "UFW turns up the heat." *Register Pajaronian*, July 22.

———. 1998b. "UFW demands a quicker pace in Coastal Berry election probe." *Santa Cruz County Sentinel*, September 15.

Meyer, John W., and Brian Rowan. 1977. "Institutionalized Organizations: Formal Structure as Myth and Ceremony." *American Journal of Sociology* 83(2):340–363.

Michels, Robert. 1915 [1911]. *Political Parties: A Sociological Study of the Oligarchical Tendencies of Modern Democracy.* Translated by Eden Paul and Cedar Paul. New York: Free Press.

Milkman, Ruth, ed. 2000. *Organizing Immigrants: The Challenge for Unions in Contemporary California.* Ithaca, NY: Cornell University Press.

Milkman, Ruth, and Kent Wong. 2001. "Organizing Immigrant Workers: Case Studies from Southern California." In L. Turner, H. C. Katz, and R. W. Hurd, eds., *Rekindling the Movement: Labor's Quest for Relevance in the 21st Century.* Ithaca, NY: Cornell University Press.

Minkoff, Debra C., and John D. McCarthy. 2005. "Reinvigorating the Study of Organizational Processes in Social Movements." *Mobilization* 10(2):289–308.

Moberg, David. 2001. "Organization Man." *The Nation,* July 16.

Mooney, Patrick H., and Theo J. Majka. 1995. *Farmers' and Farm Workers' Movements: Social Protest in American Agriculture.* New York: Twayne.

Pacini, David. 1998. "Pickers united to fight UFW." *Register Pajaronian*, July 22.

Pawel, Miriam. 2009. *The Union of Their Dreams: Power, Hope, and Struggle in Cesar Chavez's Farm Worker Movement.* New York: Bloomsbury.

Perrow, Charles. 1986. *Complex Organizations: A Critical Essay,* 3rd ed. New York: McGraw Hill.

Pitt-Rivers, Julian A. 1954. *The People of the Sierra.* Chicago: University of Chicago Press.

Portes, Alejandro, and Julia Sensenbrenner. 1993. "Embeddedness and Immigration: Notes on the Social Determinants of Economic Action. *American Journal of Sociology* 98:1320–1350.

Powell, Walter W., and Paul J. DiMaggio, eds. 1991. *The New Institutionalism in Organizational Analysis.* Chicago: University of Chicago Press.

Ramakrishnan, Karthick S., and Irene Bloemraad, eds. 2008. *Civic Hopes and Political Realities: Immigrants, Community Organizations, and Political Engagement.* New York: Russell Sage Foundation.

Rodebaugh, Dale. 1997a. "UFW rally rips ads." *San Jose Mercury News*, August 21.

———. 1997b. "Safeway backs rights for field hands." *San Jose Mercury News*, September 16.

———. 1998a. "UFW: Rival berry group a 'sham.'" *San Jose Mercury News*, July 21.

———. 1998b. "Berry union election OK'd: Vote today: Panel seeks end to violence; UFW calls group a 'sham.'" *San Jose Mercury News*, July 23.

Rubenstein, Bruce. 1998. "Trade group charges grower with union collusion." *Corporate Legal Times,* September.

Sánchez, George J. 1993. *Becoming Mexican American: Ethnicity, Culture and Identity in Chicano Los Angeles, 1900–1945.* New York: Oxford University Press.

Schlosser, Eric. 1995. "In the Strawberry Fields." *Atlantic Magazine,* November, 291–305.

Schwerin, Karl H. 1973. "The Anthropological Antecedents: Caciques, Cacicazgos, and Caciquismo." In R. Kern, ed., *The Caciques: Oligarchical Politics and the System of Caciquismo in the Luso-Hispanic World.* Albuquerque: University of New Mexico Press.

Scott, James C. 1977. "Patron Client Politics and Political Change in Southeast Asia." In S.W. Schmidt et al., eds., *Friends, Followers, and Factions: A Reader in Political Clientelism.* Berkeley: University of California Press.

Scott, W. Richard. 2008. *Institutions and Organizations: Ideas and Interests,* 3rd ed. Thousand Oaks, CA: Sage.

Shaw, Randy. *Beyond the Fields: Cesar Chavez, the UFW, and the Struggle for Justice in the 21st Century.* Berkeley: University of California Press.

Sherman, Rachel, and Kim Voss. 2000. "'Organize or Die': Labor's New Tactics and Immigrant Workers." In R. Milkman, ed., *Organizing Immigrants: The Challenge for Unions in Contemporary California.* Ithaca, NY: Cornell University Press.

Skocpol, Theda. 2003. *Diminished Democracy: From Membership to Management in American Civic Life.* Norman: University of Oklahoma Press.

Smelser, Neil J., and Richard Swedberg, eds. 2005. *The Handbook of Economic Sociology,* 2nd ed. Princeton, NJ: Princeton University Press.

Snow, David A. 2007. "Framing Processes, Ideology, and Discursive Fields." In David A. Snow, Sarah Soule, and Hanspeter Kriesi, eds., *The Blackwell Companion to Social Movements.* Oxford: Blackwell.

Soares, Joseph A. 1999. *The Decline of Privilege: The Modernization of Oxford University.* Stanford, CA: Stanford University Press.

Sotero, Ray. 1996. "Strawberry group says UFW is misleading public." *Ag Alert,* December 4.

Staggenborg, Suzanne. 1991. *The Pro-Choice Movement: Organization and Activism in the Abortion Conflict.* New York: Oxford University Press.

Stinchcombe, Arthur. 1965. "Social Structure and Organizations." In James G. March, ed., *Handbook of Organizations.* . Chicago: Rand McNally.

Stoll, Steven. 1998. *The Fruits of Natural Advantage: Making the Industrial Countryside in California.* Berkeley: University of California Press.

Swedberg, Richard. 2003. *Principles of Economic Sociology.* Princeton, NJ: Princeton University Press.

Swidler, Ann. 1986. "Culture in Action: Symbols and Strategies." *American Sociological Review* 51:273–286.

Takaki, Ronald. 1989. *Strangers from a Different Shore: a History of Asian Americans.* Boston: Little, Brown.

Tarrow, Sidney. 1988. "National Politics and Collective Action: Recent Theory and Research in Western Europe and the United States." *Annual Review of Sociology* 14:421–440.

———. 1989. *Democracy and Disorder: Protest and Politics in Italy, 1965–1975.* Oxford: Oxford University Press.

————. 1994. *Power in Movement: Social Movements, Collective Action, and Politics,* 1st ed. New York: Cambridge University Press.

Taylor, J. Edward, Philip L. Martin, and Michael Fix. 1997. *Poverty and Prosperity: Immigration and the Changing Face of Rural California.* Washington, DC: Urban Institute Press.

Thomas, Robert J. 1981. "The Social Organization of Industrial Agriculture." *Insurgent Sociologist* 10:5–20.

————. 1985. *Citizenship, Gender, and Work: Social Organization of Industrial Agriculture.* Berkeley: University of California Press.

Tilly, Charles. 1984. "Social Movements and National Politics." In Charles Bright and Susan Harding, eds., *Statemaking and Social Movements.* Ann Arbor: University of Michigan Press.

Tucker, Robert C., ed. 1978. *The Marx-Engels Reader,* 2nd ed. New York: W.W. Norton.

Turner, Lowell, Harry C. Katz, and Richard W. Hurd, eds. 2001. *Rekindling the Movement: Labor's Quest for Relevance in the 21st Century.* Ithaca, NY: Cornell University Press.

UFW. 1996. "Five Cents for Fairness. The Case for Change in the Strawberry Fields." www.ufw .org. Retrieved April 29, 2000.

————. 1998. "Salinas second Central Coast city to back UFW's strawberry workers' organizing campaign." www.ufw.org. Retrieved April 29, 2000.

————. 1999. "As strawberry pickers prepare to vote in new election, 20 berry growers and groups settle UFW suits over illegally funding 'workers committees.'" www.ufw.org. Retrieved April 29, 2000.

Villarreal, Andrés. 2002. "Political Violence and Competition in Mexico: Hierarchical Social Control in Local Patronage Structures." *American Sociological Review* 67:477–498.

Waldinger, Roger, and Michael I. Lichter. 2003. *How the Other Half Works: Immigration and the Social Organization of Labor.* Berkeley: University of California Press.

Weber, Max. 1978. *Economy and Society.* Berkeley: University of California Press.

Wells, Miriam J. 1984. "The Resurgence of Sharecropping: Historical Anomaly or Political Strategy?" *American Journal of Sociology* 90(1):1–29.

————. 1996. *Strawberry Fields: Politics, Class, and Work in California Agriculture.* Ithaca, NY: Cornell University Press.

————. 2000. "Immigration and Unionization in the San Francisco Hotel Industry." In Ruth Milkman, ed., *Organizing Immigrants: The Challenge for Unions in Contemporary California.* Ithaca, NY: Cornell University Press.

Wells, Miriam J., and Don Villarejo. 2004. "State Structures and Social Movement Strategies." *Politics and Society* 32:291–326.

Wilson, Marshall. 1997. "Raspberry pickers sue grower: 3 in Watsonville say farm didn't pay for overtime." *San Francisco Chronicle,* August 8.

Wilson, William Julius. 1980. *The Declining Significance of Race: Blacks and Changing American Institutions,* 2nd ed. Chicago: University of Chicago Press.

Wolf, Eric R. 1966. "Kinship, Friendship, and Patron-Client Relations in Complex Societies." In Michael Banton, ed., *The Social Anthropology of Complex Societies.* London: Tavistock.

Wolf, Eric R., and Edward Hansen. 1967. "Caudillo Politics: Structural Analysis." *Comparative Studies in Society and History* 9:168–179.

Wong, Janelle S. 2006. *Democracy's Promise: Immigrants and American Civic Institutions.* Ann Arbor: University of Michigan Press.

Zald, Mayer N., and John D. McCarthy. 1987. *Social Movements in an Organizational Society.* New Brunswick, NJ: Transaction.

Index

About the Book

Gilbert Mireles explores the legendary United Farm Workers' campaign to organize laborers—predominantly Latino immigrants—in California's strawberry industry.

Tracing the UFW's actions from the picking fields to the world of government offices and corporate boardrooms, Mireles shows how the very traits that made the union such a successful advocate for farm workers also inhibited the meaningful participation of those same workers in the union. His systematic analysis of one of the most influential social movements in the country points to troubling implications for the place of immigrants—and the role of civil society and participatory democracy—in US society.

Gilbert Felipe Mireles is assistant professor of sociology at Whitman College.